Building Green *in a Black and White World*

A Guide to Selling the Homes Your Customers Want

David Johnston

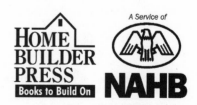

Home Builder Press®
National Association of Home Builders
1201 15th Street, NW
Washington, DC 20005-2800
(800) 223-2665
www.builderbooks.com

Building Green in a Black and White World: A Guide to Selling the Homes Your Customers Want
ISBN 0-86718-507-4

Cover and text design by Rajan Kose, Standing Stone Design
Printed in the United States of America on recycled paper

Library of Congress Cataloging-in-Publication Data
Johnston, David Robert.
    Building green in a black and white world: selling the homes your customers want/
    David Johnston.
        p.   cm.
    Includes bibliographical references.
    ISBN 0-86718-507-4
    1. House construction. 2. Building materials–Environmental aspects. 3. Green products.
    4. Dwellings–Marketing. I. Title
TH4812 .J64 1999
690'.8'0688–dc21   99-050359
                                                                                CIP

Disclaimer:
    The information and opinions described in this book on green building are based on the building philosophy and experience of the author, David Johnston. They do not necessarily represent the policy nor the opinions of NAHB or its staff. While the book acknowledges some of the exciting new green building concepts being used in the industry today, it does not purport to cover every possible technique used nationwide for building green. In addition, while regional differences are mentioned throughout the book, those described are by no means exhaustive of the many standards and practices currently in use throughout the country.
    The publication of this book does not constitute an explicit or implicit endorsement by the National Association of Home Builders or Home Builder Press of any specific technique or policy. Furthermore, neither NAHB nor Home Builder Press makes any representation as to the effectiveness or validity of any of the techniques and opinions discussed in this book. Finally, NAHB hereby disclaims any and all liability that may arise from the use of this book or its contents.

For more information please contact:
    Home Builder Press®
    National Association of Home Builders
    1201 15th Street, NW
    Washington, DC 20005-2800
    (800) 223-2665
    http://www.nahb.com/builderbooks

Additional copies of this publication are available from Home Builder Press. NAHB members receive a 20 percent member discount on publications purchased through Home Builder Press. Quantity discounts also are available.

12/99 Standing Stone Design/Data Reproductions Inc. 2000

Contents

Section 1 - Why Build Green?

Section 2 - Becoming a Green Builder

Section 3 - Sales and Marketing

Appendices

Acknowledgments

Acknowledgments fall into several categories. There are those who know who they are and those who have been guiding lights for my life.

To my mentors, without whom I would never have come this far, I am forever grateful: Bob Prentice who taught me to build plumb and square; Paul Kando who taught me that nothing is impossible; Fred Morse who taught me that the sun shines every day whether we see it or not; Bob Naismith who taught me that the only way to do business is with integrity; Derek Havens who taught me that it is easier to pull a string than to push it; Bill Reed who taught me the meaning of compassionate, visionary architecture; Tom Hoyt for being the booster rocket engine of my career; Jim Kenny who continually shows me that one man can change the world; David Adamson who is my model of commitment and tenacity; and especially my wife Elena for her constant support and wisdom.

To those without whom this book would never have become a reality: Megan Murdock, steady as a rock and smart as a whip; Jayn Stewart, editor extraordinaire and dear friend; and Rajan Kose of Standing Stone Design with the design eye of an eagle and the heart of an elephant. Many thanks to the visionary activists within NAHB who have kept green building in front of the industry: Ron Jones, Chair of the Green Building Sub-committee; Peter Yost at NAHB-RC; and Neil Gaffney at NAHB headquarters; and particularly to Kurt Lindblom and the staff of Home Builder Press whose vision and good-hearted support delivered all of us to the distant shore of publication.

My gratitude to those pioneers who have lit my way and who are creating the future with intention. R. Buckminster Fuller who changed my life and will eventually change the planet; Bruce Goff for his courage to express the inner world through architecture; Doug Balcomb for making passive solar architecture go beyond engineering; Ray Anderson for his commitment and outspoken will to achieve a sustainable future; Mikhail Gorbachev and Global Green for making the future one of peace and environmental justice; Bill Browning and RMI for making sustainability a reality.

And finally, Lynn Simon, Amy Townsend, Marc Richmond-Powers, Claudine Schneider, Doug Parker, for their love, contributions, and support through this endeavor.

Building Green in a Black and White World: A Guide to Selling the Homes Your Customers Want was produced under the general direction of Tom Downs, NAHB Executive Vice President and CEO, in association with Bob Brown, Vice President of Knowledge Management; Adrienne Ash, Assistant Staff Vice President, Publishing Services; Charlotte McKamy, Publisher; Kurt Lindblom, Acquisitions Editor and Project Manager; David Rhodes, Art Director; Jayn Stewart, Copyeditor; and Maryanne Orloff, Proofreader.

About the Author

David Johnston is president of What's Working, an international environmental design and consulting firm in Boulder, Colorado, specializing in environmental construction technology. He is a past director of the Boulder, Colorado Home Builder's Association and coauthor of the Denver Metro HBA Green Builder Certification Program. He has also developed green builder programs for the cities of Boulder and Aspen in Colorado, and the City of Los Angeles. He is currently developing new green building guidelines for Alameda County, the East Bay Area of San Francisco. What's Working developed a marketing strategy for the U.S. Green Building Council to introduce the nation's first commercial building environmental rating system, Leadership in Energy and Environmental Design (LEED).

What's Working has been selected to represent the United States at International Energy Agency meetings to develop international research in the area of sustainable buildings.

Founder in 1980 of the Passive Solar Industries Council in Washington, D.C. (in which the National Association of Home Builders was a founding member), Johnston also created his own construction company, Lightworks Construction. Lightworks was named one of the top 50 contractors in the country in 1990 by Remodeling Magazine.

Johnston is currently a columnist for the *Boulder Daily Camera* with a monthly "Building Green" column. In addition, he has been published in *Builder Magazine*, *Remodeling Magazine*, *Professional Builder*, *Fine Home Building*, *Home Energy* and other national publications. What's Working has been featured in articles in the *Wall Street Journal*, *Washington Post*, *San Francisco Examiner*, *Chicago Tribune*, *The New York Times*, and many other newspapers.

Named the Associate Member of the Year by the Boulder HBA, Johnston also received the 1996 Environmental Business of the Year Award from the Boulder Chamber of Commerce. In addition, he was inducted into the Built Green Hall of Fame by the Denver HBA in 1997 and in 1998 was awarded the prestigious University of Colorado Corporate Excellence Award for Sustainable Development.

Johnston currently consults with developers, architects, builders, and homeowners internationally in energy-efficient, environmentally friendly housing.

Several years ago, while working on a large custom home in Santa Fe, a couple of the members of my crew and I found ourselves trying to figure out how to best secure a large piece of flagstone to an adobe wall. The wall was inside the dining room, and the stone was being mounted vertically. It would serve as the background material from which a bronze figure would be hung. We eventually found an acceptable way to attach the stone to the adobe, and it hangs there to this day, serving the purpose for which it was intended.

What struck us at the time was the irony of the situation. We were engaged in building a state-of-the-art custom home in one of the premier markets in the country, and we found ourselves attempting to stick a rock onto a mud wall! We laughed at the time and joked that pretty soon we would be putting people back into caves and painting decorations on the walls by torchlight.

In truth, that exercise was no different from any of the thousands of other procedures we completed in the construction of that building. It just happened to involve some basic materials. Our clients wanted to include that particular combination in order to satisfy a desire. And while it demanded much less technology than other features, it still required our full attention and expertise.

While the use of materials like stone and adobe are to some extent symbolic, I am convinced that we find ourselves coming full circle in terms of what we build and how we build it. Every day more emphasis is given to appropriate technologies, materials, and practices. Our clients are demanding buildings that enjoy a sense of place, that blend the organic with the technological, buildings that feel as though they have "grown" where they are.

Green building is no longer the province of starry-eyed visionaries in Birkenstocks who dream of the day when financing will exist to allow them to build their own straw bale castles. Mainstream builders are coming to terms with what they have intuitively known all along: that responsible and careful use of all building resources is essential if we intend to build into the future.

I am honored to have the opportunity to make this modest statement of encouragement to those who would read this book. Many of the real heroes of the sustainability movement are included in the following pages. David Johnston has managed to craft a message that is immensely readable and enjoyable, yet equally rich and varied in content. Use it wisely. Find ways to include this information in your daily work.

Our company measures the success or failure of our projects by what we call the "element of undeniability." Simply stated, a project is successful for us if we can honestly say that what we have constructed is undeniably appropriate in its location, its material components, and its use of technology. Perhaps that is just another way of saying it's green.

Ron Jones
Chair of NAHB Green Building Sub-Committee
Sierra Custom Builders
Placitas, New Mexico

This book has been kicking around inside me for twenty years. I have always been involved with my environment. From the time I was a kid in the suburbs of Chicago, I spent most of my time after school in the woods and prairies. I lived outdoors, catching insects, taming raccoons, and fishing in the local streams and ponds. I reveled in the way nature changed throughout the year from spring green to summer lush to fall leaves to winter silence.

Tree Houses

In my mind, wooded areas were made for building forts and tree houses. Somehow they were never complete, so I kept on building. The highlight of high school was building a three-story tree house in a giant elm tree way off in the woods. Three of us worked on it during summers after football practice and on cold fall afternoons. Building that tree house fulfilled me as nothing else did. My friends and I planned and improvised and found thrown-away materials we could use. Then we built like banshees until the pictures in our heads stood in physical reality before us. After a long weekend of work, I'd look back and feel great about what we had accomplished. One of the best features of the tree house was that we could get away from the grown-ups at will. Thirty feet up and hidden in a dense forest, they couldn't find us, and if they

did, they couldn't get to us! That tree house was big enough to sleep six couples in relative privacy on prom night, much to the chagrin of our parents.

Life Before Bucky

When I went to college in 1968 at the University of Colorado, I thought that engineering would be the key to continuing my building experience. I bent my mind around calculus and physics and statistics and structures, but it was all too abstract. I missed the practical experience of building. I missed nailing boards together. So in the summers I worked on construction sites. It was there that my real learning took place.

College and I parted ways after three-and-a-half years so that I could return to building houses. I thought my tree house and summer building projects would be all the experience I needed to become a carpenter in the "real" world. Was I ever wrong! I had no idea there were such dues to be paid! The builders I met were renegades, and young bucks, like me, were minions to be ordered into servitude. "Boy, see that pile of 2x4s over there? They need to be over here. Go move 'em and see me when you're done." After two long hours of hauling boards, I heard, "Boy what are you doing? Those 2x4s are in the way! Move 'em back to where they were, pronto!"

College days started to look sweeter and sweeter.

Black and White Rules

My savior was a great man named Bob Prentice. He was a third generation Colorado carpenter whose granddaddy had built bars in Cripple Creek during the gold rush days. Bob was a compassionate perfectionist. He taught me a lesson I had never learned in my twenty-something years. There is only one way to do things . . . right! If it went up, it was plumb. If it went across, it was level. When boards came together, they were square. Period. "Half a bubble out of plumb" was reserved for descriptions of the mentality of our laborers.

I am grateful to Bob to this day because while the rest of the world was saying, "Good enough is good enough," Bob challenged me to build it right. What a concept! What if that philosophy of doing it right was applied to the rest of my life? What would that look like? My entire life I had been searching for black and white rules to follow that would always be true—Bob gave me the first chapter in the rulebook.

I followed in Bob's bar-building family tradition and moved to Mississippi to build three bars in a college town. I jumped all over the chance to design and build commercial spaces without being a licensed architect or contractor. Each of the three buildings was unique. We used recycled stained glass, turned balusters, and wrought iron salvaged from torn down antebellum mansions.

Design was now in my blood. Drawing pictures and creating three-dimensional constructions, from paper to completion, was thrilling. I wanted more.

Life After Bucky

A client retained me to design and build a geodesic dome country retreat. I had never built one, but I knew that the inventor, Buckminster Fuller, fondly known as Bucky, was teaching at Southern Illinois University. The design school at the university taught classes in constructing geodesic domes, so I decided to go to the source for the information I needed. When I arrived in Carbondale, Illinois, in 1974, I knew that my life would be different from that point forward. In one geodesic dome that had been converted into a workshop, I saw an electric vehicle being built on a VW chassis. It was one of the first hybrid designs to get over sixty miles per gallon. In another shop, carcasses of wind machines were being rebuilt using contemporary electrical technology. These machines would be given to local families after their resurrection. Site-built solar panels were everywhere. I was home! I started school a month later. The Design Science program required that you create your own major so I invented what I called "Environmental Systems Design."

Life took on a new reference point for me: there was life before Bucky, and life after Bucky. From day one, my thinking was challenged and changed. We were taught to think in systems. Any object, place, or thought was made up of sub-systems and was a part of a meta-system, or larger context. All systems were created equally. They all followed the same rules, at least in theory. Smaller systems and larger systems dynamically interacted constantly. Nothing had meaning in isolation. It made so much sense! Everything was connected—like nature. Nothing existed separately from anything else. A shift in one place affected the equilibrium of everything else.

Systems thinking became part of my daily life. In order to study buildings, I had to learn about urban planning and forest ecology.

And how could I understand heating and cooling systems without a solid background in climatology and human comfort conditions? (The term "passive solar" had not been coined yet. It was called "applied climatology!")

So many interrelationships became obvious to me. A building was an integral part of its surrounding ecosystem. If it respected the ecosystem and interacted with the natural flows, everything functioned better. Either it fit systemically or it was an irritant to the larger system. Buildings that interrupted animal habitats or changed water courses or microclimatic conditions had larger systemic impacts than just at the site itself. A building also had significant impact on the occupants, for good or ill. I learned that drafting an architectural wonder was unacceptable unless its existence was environmentally justified.

Applied Common Sense

I graduated with my degree in Environmental Systems Design. Each word held a special significance for me. Designing environmental systems was a delightful challenge. Solar heating, wind-generated electrical energy, hybrid electric vehicles, and structures that danced with the elements all stimulated my thinking, my imagination, and my soul.

The horizons of my thinking said that systems were the basis of understanding everything. With systems thinking we could redevelop cities; we could eliminate environmental pollution; we could even cure cancer. It was all just a design opportunity. Take what works today and redesign the rest. It was all so logical—applied common sense. I also developed a new appreciation for architects. I assumed that they knew what good design was because they had gone through the kind of training that I had. Architects had to know and synthesize an amazing amount of information to be able to design buildings that worked on so many levels.

After graduation, my optimism led me to believe that it was just a matter of time until all design would be based on environmental systems. I wanted to be on the cutting edge of this exciting time. I was sure a new dawn was emerging that would shape how we built buildings from now on. Environmentally responsive, solar powered, human engineered, esthetically integrated—the home of the twenty-first century had arrived twenty-five years ahead of schedule! Environmentalists had predicted that we would hit our limits to growth in the year 2000, but with this new vision we were going to make it! We had the tools, and the world would obviously understand its dilemma and transform itself for the sake of the future. Once again, I believed I had a clear view of the black and white rules of the game.

Reclaiming My Tool Belt

Many years and many miles later, I realized how woefully inaccurate my assumptions had been. What I had thought was inevitable (a world based on systems thinking, renewable energy, and human engineering) never truly came to pass. Solar had a short life in the late '70s and early '80s. Geodesic domes made great radar enclosures for the defense department, but they never

made it to the suburbs. Bucky died in 1983, loved but not understood. Clear guiding principles seemed to get lost in the oil embargo and the subsequent recession.

Trying to recapture the enthusiasm of my early tree house days, I designed homes, taught college, consulted for the government, and ran a construction industry trade association. But something was missing, something about looking over my shoulder at the end of the day and feeling gratified at seeing the frame of a new structure that wasn't there days ago. Building was still in my blood....

In 1983, I started a construction company in Washington, D.C., called Lightworks Construction. I wanted this company to combine the solar work I had done and the construction I loved. We were going to design and build solar homes that would embody all the principles I had learned in school with the latest state-of-the-art passive solar design. I expected that by just letting the world know we existed, customers would flock to our door.

I learned quickly that the construction world didn't work that way. We built lots of projects, but they were fairly conventional. Starter homes, refinished basements, and additions weren't getting us to where we wanted to be. I started to realize that we were competing for jobs with every Tom, Dick, and Harry with a pick-up truck and a dog in the back.

We had no clear identity in the marketplace. If we wanted to do something different, we needed to let the world know we were different. We had been doing business by the book, following all the black and white rules of starting a construction company. But what I realized was that I didn't want a black and white company, I wanted a "green" construction company! Black and white felt normal, average, and invisible. All this time I had thought if I just played by the black and white rules, I could win the game. But I really didn't want to play that game at all. Everything I cared about was green, not black and white! I didn't want to build typical houses that looked like all the others on the block. I wanted to build houses that incorporated all I had learned about systems, energy efficiency, and quality construction that would last a hundred years.

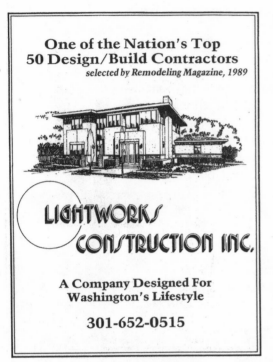

One of the Nation's Top 50 Design/Build Contractors
selected by Remodeling Magazine, 1989

LIGHTWORKS CONSTRUCTION INC.

A Company Designed For Washington's Lifestyle

301-652-0515

We discussed all this at Lightworks and decided to make some changes. We needed to be bold in order to make an impact. To differentiate ourselves from other builders, we created an identity based on the energy and environmental features we offered. We hired marketing and advertising consultants, a graphic designer, and media consultants. We identified our markets geographically and demographically. We put money into publicity that promoted our green image, emphasizing the design/build aspect of our company. We showed that we were concerned with energy conservation and solar. Our efforts to differentiate ourselves in the market created immediate results: we got more calls in a month than we had in all of the previous year!

Our success continued for the next seven years. We grew, built beautiful projects, and became the contractor of the year in Washington, D.C. We were named one of the top fifty contractors in the country by *Remodeling Magazine*. They selected Lightworks because of how we did business, how we marketed ourselves, and how we treated our clients. Building green in a black and white world paid off in spades!

Doing Well by Doing Good

That experience taught me that success comes from taking risks. Building is risky business in itself, but *true* risk is putting one's values on the line. To say, "This is what I believe in, and this is how I do it," is a tough position to take in a world where many rewards seem to be based on playing the game and not rocking the boat.

Real success, though, can come from first playing the game by the rules (doing good business, watching the bottom line, taking care of employees, treating customers with respect), then making up new rules that achieve a high- er result. Building "true and plumb" became not only a maxim in my construction company, but a standard by which we did business. We treated everyone fairly, we built projects on a handshake, and we created win-win opportunities for everyone we worked with. Integrity became our company motto. If a carpenter was sweeping out the job after a hard day of cutting and sanding, he did it with the same care he used in putting up crown molding.

There is an old expression, "doing well by doing good." We not only did good work, we did good by our clients. We worked closely with them. And if the job didn't cost as much as we estimated, we would refund their money. We opened our books so clients knew exactly what

EXCELLENCE IN PROFESSIONAL REMODELING

THE BIG 50

This year's Big 50 remodelers have achieved excellence in design, marketing, business and team management. They run successful big businesses and small businesses. They are growing rapidly, and thriving in particular market niches.

RISING STARS

These remodelers are on the rise. In a relatively short time they have made their marks in the industry. And with progressive, well-run businesses, they are poised to grow.

LIGHTWORKS CONSTRUCTION INC.
Bethesda, Md.

"Quality, integrity and ser- vice" roll off David John- ston's tongue when he ex- plains his company's success. "We try to look at business as an extension of life. We take the rules that work for us in- terpersonally and apply them to our relationships with our customers."

Lightworks is character- ized by extremely strong fi- nancial management, innova- tive business systems and Johnston's philosophical base. Vice president Derek Havens says, "Within our strong busi- ness structure, we encourage people to have fun, innovate and show creativity to spur the accomplishing of their jobs." It's a formula that serves them well.

Residential and commercial design-build remodeler
8 years in business
1988 volume: $1 million
Staff: 7 office, 18 field

DAVID JOHNSTON, DEREK HAVENS

Reprinted from the May 1989 issue of REMODELING magazine, copyright © Hanley-Wood, Inc.

their home cost. That way, if the job ran over, they were more will- ing to cover the overages. Our clients became our best salespeo- ple. They would refer us with such enthusiasm that we often did- n't compete for new work. Their friends wanted us, and that was that. We also did good for the environment. We built to last. We built homes that used one half as much energy as our competi- tion. Our clients loved our attention to detail, especially to the details of how they wanted to live their lives.

What's Working

I started What's Working, my environmental construction consulting firm, in 1992 to assist construction companies in making the transition to a sustainable future. I have worked with dozens of developers, builders, architects, and homeowners to create over 500 healthy, environmentally friendly homes and buildings. This on-the-ground experience of consulting on a wide variety of buildings provided the foundation for creating green building certification programs across the country. In seven years of training and speaking, I have worked with hundreds of builders from coast-to-coast. Green building is a great way of expressing, through business, a value that most of us hold dear—the quality of life in our hometowns.

Building Green in a Black and White World brings together systems thinking, green building, and market research, all of which can result in the kind of houses your customers want. The bottom line is that green building is just good business.

It is my attempt in this book to show how we can start to take the future into our own hands. Green building is about creating the future with intention: the intention to build a better world for our children and our children's children. By taking a leadership role and creating green homes that are gentle on the planet and healthy for our clients, we can help reverse past environmental damage. I believe that all of us want to make the world a better place. The same is true of our customers. Green building is an "applied common sense" kind of solution that has its roots based in the wisdom of our forefathers. These master builders erected strong buildings hundreds of years ago that are still here today. Through thoughtful placement on the land, wise use of water, incorporating natural energy, and building healthy environments for our children, we as builders can help create a flourishing planet for those growing up behind us.

David Johnston
What's Working
Boulder, Colorado
October, 1999

This is a book about thinking differently while doing many of the same things you have always done. It isn't a "how to build" book, although there will be many "how-to's" sprinkled throughout. You will see how green building can improve your bottom line while providing the kind of housing your customers want.

A green building does everything a house has always done, and it can even look the same from the street, but it is inherently different. From foundations to finishes, green building substitutes improve quality and add value for the homebuyer.

More importantly, green building is the market of the future. It provides an opportunity for forward-looking builders to be the first in their market to embrace the principles of energy efficiency, healthy indoor environments, and resource conservation. By building green, you can differentiate yourself from the competition and build homes that are more attractive to buyers. How do you know that a green home is what homebuyers are looking for? Because these homes are often healthier, quieter, more affordable, and more comfortable. They can also require less maintenance than conventional homes. Ask prospective homebuyers if these qualities are important to them and find out!

Increasing numbers of Americans consider themselves environmentalists. (As you will see in Chapter 1.) They are recycling seven times more stuff today than they did ten years ago. They are buying organic vegetables and recycled paper products. Environmental consumerism is one of the fastest-growing segments in the marketplace. Buying green homes is a logical next step in this national trend.

Today, most builders are building green without knowing it. Because most of the green building products were developed to function better than their conventional counterparts, many of these products are already in use. For example, engineered lumber products were once exclusively in the domain of commercial construction. As the products became more available and the price started coming down, they were used in high-end residential construction. Now they are used for most residential construction projects. Their positive environmental story, however, is rarely used as a sales tool.

For example, wood I-joists are now increasingly replacing 2x10s or 2x12s for floors and ceilings. A 2x10 (or larger) generally requires an old growth tree to be cut down, which places pressure on national forests for logging. A wood I-joist uses different wood species for the major components of the material. Oriented strand board (OSB) used for the web of the truss can be made of aspen. By using wood I-joists, more of the tree can be used. And it requires only 50 percent as much wood fiber as solid-sawn lumber. For children who are learning about forest ecology in school, this use becomes a graphic illustration of the positive impact of green building.

Wood I-joists are stronger and lighter than 2x10s and 2x12s, and they never need to be "crowned." They can be installed more efficiently, thereby reducing labor costs and producing a floor that will never squeak from warping joists.

This is the point of the book: You can build green, but if you don't tell your customers the benefits, they may never know and may never care. Once your marketing supports your material choices and the specifications of your project, you can differentiate yourself in the marketplace. And you will sell more homes to increasingly discerning buyers.

In a workshop for builders on building green I took a poll around the room. I asked builders to tell me what differentiated them in the marketplace. One builder after another stood up and said, "We build quality and value into every home we build." By the fifth or sixth time, it became obvious that there was little differentiation in the room! One of the last builders stood up and said, "I build environmentally friendly homes that have demonstrably better quality and higher value, not only to the homebuyer, but to the planet as well." He stood out like a sore thumb in the room and also in his market.

In the marketing world an old maxim is, "Sell the sizzle, not the steak." Green marketing is a way to sell environmental sizzle in ways you typically might never think of. Energy efficiency can be a yawn in the marketplace. Solar by itself has hardly sold a house in a decade. But in the context of green building, they become major selling points in the overall environmental story.

Your customers want you to take the lead in making their largest investment a statement of their personal values. They trust you to provide the best product you know how to build. John Knott developer of Dewees Island, South Carolina, once said, "If you went to the doctor for open heart surgery and he told you he selected all the nurses, instruments, and surgical equipment from the low cost bidder, would you entrust him with your life?" Your buyers are entrusting you with their lives in a similar way. Wouldn't you rather tell them that you have different criteria for your decisions than the competition and that you are building the best home you can possibly build in their behalf?

This book is about how to step up to the plate and take the challenge to build homes that make a difference to your customers and to the environment at the same time.

In my thirty years in the building industry, I have witnessed the evolution of the market for green building. I have seen firsthand the change in consumer demands for homes that reflect their values and lifestyles. The builders I have worked with over the last seven years tell me that green building has become a milestone in creating success and profit in their business. It is my hope that the information in this book can help you do the same.

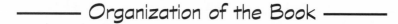

Organization of the Book

Section One

This section answers the question: "Why build green?"

Chapter 1 focuses on the market, consumer trends, and consumer desires for environmentally considerate products.

Chapter 2 shows the context for green homes and the big picture environmental issues that are the "drivers" for the long-term market.

If you are familiar with the basics of green building you might want to jump right into Section Two for "how-tos" and come back to Section One for references.

Section Two

This section answers the question: "How can I become a green builder?"

Chapter 3 shows you how to enter the market, step by step. You will learn about the issues, the costs, and the process to get you started.

Chapter 4 guides you through the process of becoming a green business and getting participation from your employees and trades contractors.

Section Three

This section answers the question: "How can I successfully market and sell green homes?" You will see how other builders have used innovative sales and marketing approaches that have been highly successful.

Chapter 5 shows you how to turn green building into a "marketing bonanza," as a builder in Austin, Texas, calls it.

Chapter 6 takes you step-by-step through selling your homes in ways your customers will get excited about.

Chapter 7 gives you case studies that can assist you in selling green.

Appendicies

The appendicies provide handy references and resources for more in-depth information.

Appendix A outlines six HBA programs and gives you the checklists from four of those programs.

Appendix B provides resource information: reading list, web sites, organizations and HBA Green Builder program contacts.

Appendix C is a bibliography.

Symbols

Throughout the book look for these two symbols which provide a quick way to get to the meat of a section and guide you to the how-tos and to cautionary choice points.

 Action Arrows represent actions you can take.

 Caution Symbols are things to pay attention to.

1

What The Market Tells Us

This chapter brings together current market research relevant to green building.

Knowing Your Market - Demographic studies of consumers show the connections between environmental concern and consumer behavior.

Trends Related to Green Building - Consumer surveys show mounting interest in the benefits of living in green homes and professional surveys reveal increased emphasis on green building by architects and builders.

Marketing Suggestions Based on Current Consumer Behavior - The information from this chapter's surveys can enhance your marketing efforts.

Conducting Your Own Market Research - Researching your local market is not only critical, but it is easier than you might imagine.

Building green is more about people than it is about technology. Since so much emphasis has been placed on the technology of green building, this book has been designed to help you shift your focus. For many of your potential customers, the benefits of green building (providing healthier environments both inside and out) evoke images of happy children now and in the future. With this in mind, the key to becoming a successful green builder is communicating with your customers how and why you build green.

Surveys show that Americans are increasingly interested in living a healthy lifestyle and in preserving the quality of life in their communities. The good news for builders is that the market for green homes couldn't be better. You only have to look as far as your grocery store to see evidence of the changing market. Fresh vegetable salad bars are springing up everywhere, and organic produce is the fastest-growing segment of the food industry.

Green building meets the public where they live. Many market research surveys, including the *Wall Street Journal*, show that the vast majority of Americans (consistently over 75 percent) consider themselves environmentalists. They are concerned about impacts on the environment that they see around them. Whether these impacts take the form of traffic jams, beaches closing, or the brown clouds that grow each year over their cities, the public wants to preserve their natural world. Choosing to buy a green home allows them to take an active role in counteracting these concerns. The more educated the public is about green homes, the more likely they are to buy green.

Bill Eich,
Bill Eich Construction Co., Inc.
Spirit Lake, Iowa
(712) 336-4438
Bill Eich's construction company designs and builds six to ten new custom homes each year, doing all their own carpentry. In addition to custom homes, Eich does some commercial work and builds four to eight unit condos each year. For his excellence in remodeling work, Eich was named to Remodeling Magazine's Hall of Fame in 1996. Eich also received an award from Popular Science magazine in 1992, for the Best New Feature in Housing Technology for his frost protected shallow foundation technique.

Building green is all about meeting your buyers' desires with a product that reflects what they want out of life: health, comfort, and time to just simply relax. Builders who have responded to this changing market have prospered and claim they will never build the way they once did. In the words of Bill Eich, a custom builder in Spirit Lake, Iowa: "Green building brings a sense of pride back into construction. We consider ourselves 'born again' builders. We have reinvented how we build. We see the light and want to convert all the builders we can because it is so much better."

Bill's story: "Our process has evolved since 1984, when we first started building 'high-tech' homes. We incorporated current building science using a systems approach to construction. The benefits were immediate. The carpenters could see the difference and knew why they were doing things differently. We were improving the quality of the homes. The performance was so dramatic that it was a no-brainer to incorporate green techniques into our building process. We got such positive feedback from customers that we started including these energy-conserving features in every home. Our core crew said they wouldn't build the old way. The old way didn't make sense anymore. Everybody in the company became sold on the new approach to building. When everybody in the company is sold on it, it is easier to sell to the customer."

As the market research in this chapter reveals, and as you probably know from your own experiences, people care deeply about the health of their families, they always want to save money where they can, and they want to contribute to something greater than themselves. Green building meets these desires by reducing the amount of health compromising chemicals used in a home, by improving energy efficiency and thus reducing electric and gas bills, and by offering a practical way for people to contribute to preserving the quality of the environment through reduced resource consumption.

Market research shows that a demand exists for environmentally designed homes that is not yet being met. Good business sense tells us that fulfilling a previously unmet need translates into profit. Becoming a green builder is not only a way to generate profit in the short run, but it can ensure the future of your company.

Danny Buck, President
Living Structures, Inc.
Santa Fe, New Mexico
(505) 988-2202
Danny Buck's company, Living Structures, Inc., is a design, construction, and landscaping firm, owned by six partners and employing fifty people. Living Structures does most of its work in new single family homes, remodeling, and additions. The company also does some commercial work, including a focus on indoor air quality in doctors' offices and grocery stores. Living Structures builds with alternative wall systems such as straw bale and adobe. Currently, much of their work is with high-end clients, but they are planning on moving into the low-income market and applying green principles there.

As Santa Fe, New Mexico, builder Danny Buck puts it, "Green building is where the market is headed. I'm 100 percent convinced of it. It's not a matter of *if* there is a market for green homes, but *when* are you going to meet it? I think it is inevitable. The question is, do you want to lead the market or follow your competition? You can choose to be knowledgeable or ignorant. Which do you want to be? It's time to get on board now."

By the end of this chapter you should have a grasp of national market trends, the types of consumers most likely to be interested in a green home, and what other builders and architects see in the future for green building. From the information gained in these surveys, I will make some suggestions about how to approach marketing your green homes. Chapter 6, "Marketing Strategies," will address the topic in greater detail.

Knowing Your Market

No aspect of your customers' lives is more value-driven than their decision to purchase a home. People want their homes to reflect their values. Since a majority of Americans consider themselves environmentalists, by choosing to build green, you communicate to your customers that you understand their values. Through building green, you can sell your homes on a more personal level. Rather than simply selling the ceramic tile in the foyer or the finished basement, you are selling health, comfort, and well-being to your customers and their children.

Even with the market demand, *Building Green in a Black and White World* isn't going to pay off unless you also learn to market green. While your customers' desires for health, saving money, and improving the environment motivate their purchasing decisions, you have to show them that your homes help them meet those goals. It is important to identify your market: Who is most likely to buy a green home? What is the best way to communicate with this segment of the population? What other values, besides green, are important to them? To meet their needs effectively, you need to know how they want to live, how their values influence their purchase decisions, and what they are trying to express to the world through their home. Taking the time to know the needs and desires of your clients leads to improved sales and greater customer satisfaction. Don't assume that you know what home-buyers want based on past sales. It is always worth the effort to do some local market research.

For example, in Denver, focus groups on urban design features were conducted for the conversion of the old Stapleton Airport into a residential development project. The designers assumed that mimicking the traditional urban design of the surrounding neighborhoods, like putting the garage behind the house and adding front porches on the street side, would be a positive design improvement. The client, though, insisted on a market research test. A series of focus groups was conducted with past buyers, current shoppers, and realtors. The results were not what the designers expected.

The respondents fell into three distinct categories: the city escapees, the nostalgics, and the climbers. The first group, **the city escapees**, didn't want anything that resembled their current neighborhood or the one in which they grew up. They thought of alleys as dangerous and didn't like houses to be close together. Yards were not necessarily perceived as safe places for their children to play in. This group associated success with a suburban setting on a cul-de-sac. And the garage in front was definitely a status symbol.

The **nostalgics** had the opposite reaction. They missed the neighborhood they grew up in. For them, front porches added to a sense of community, and they yearned to be able to borrow a cup of sugar from their next door neighbor. Tall trees and shaded yards were valuable to them. Nostalgics wanted to walk to commercial centers and talk to neighbors along the way. The garage in front didn't matter at all.

The **climbers'** most pressing desire was for prestige, so they wanted a neighborhood with larger houses than their current home. They also wanted to display their new car in front of the house because the first impression from the curb was of prime importance. Open floor plans with large areas for entertainment pleased the climbers. They were not particularly interested in neighborhood social contacts and doubted they would ever use a front porch. Clearly, no single approach to site development would please all three groups!

All too often builders make the assumption that they know their market based on past sales. This can easily lead to dead ends and houses that don't move as well as the houses across the street which include innovations that are more attractive to buyers. Conducting market research, as the above example shows, is key to the success of any new project. National market research is useful to get a sense of large-scale changes in demographics and consumer interest, but all markets are essentially local. You need to know what homebuyers in your area want. The end of this chapter shows you how to conduct your own local market research.

Trends Related to Green Building

All indicators tell us that consumer behavior toward green building is changing rapidly. The following studies present a snapshot of some interesting trends.

Environmentally Conscious Consumer Behavior (ECCB)

Environmentally conscious consumer behavior indicates how people's purchasing decisions are influenced by their concern for the environment. While the following surveys were conducted as part of market research on general consumer trends, each survey offers insight to ECCB. Because green building is not only a new marketing concept, but also requires comprehending and accepting a wide range of environmental ideas, its market is not fully encompassed by these studies. Nevertheless, the predominant attitudes and the effect of these attitudes on purchasing decisions are relevant to understanding the green building market.

General Consumer Behavior

> **Surveys Used:**
>
> 1. *Cone Roper Cause Related Marketing Trends Report,* 1997.
>
> 2. *American Demographics: The Integral Culture,* Paul Ray for the Institute of Noetic Sciences and The Fetzer Institute, 1997.
>
> 3. *American Demographics: "The Integral Culture,"* Paul Ray for the Institute of Noetic Sciences and The Fetzer Institute, 1997.

Cone Roper Cause Related Marketing Trends Report (1997) strongly suggests that the American public's interest in environmental issues and corporate responsibility is on the rise. According to this report, the public ranks environmental issues as the number two area that businesses should work hardest to resolve. And they want businesses to focus on these issues locally, rather than at the national or global level. Statistics gathered in the Cone-Roper survey indicate that 76 percent of Americans would switch to a retail store associated with a good cause, such as Home Depot's decision to sell sustainably harvested lumber, when price and quality of the merchandise offered are equal. (This represents a 14 percent increase since 1996.) This statistic suggests that green building needs to be priced right for the public to buy.

American Demographics studies show that a major change is occurring in American culture toward a comprehensive shift in values, worldview, and ways of life. Three distinct worldviews are identified below.

- **Traditionalism (also known as Heartlanders):** a conservative, faith-based worldview, which dominated the early days of the United States (29 percent of Americans).

- **Modernism:** the mainstream that emerged from the industrial revolution; became the dominant paradigm early in the twentieth century. Modernists believe that progress and the good life are defined by increasing material wealth. They highly regard technology as a solution to environmental, social, and economic problems (47 percent of Americans).

• **Trans Modernism (also called Cultural Creatives):** began to emerge in the 1970s. This group believes that society faces significant problems and needs to reinvent its culture, institutions, and practices to solve problems and to provide a positive future for its children. Creatives are integrating their values into their everyday lives and are taking action on a wide range of social, environmental, and spiritual concerns (24 percent of Americans).

Because they are taking action on environmental concerns, Creatives are the logical target group for green building marketing. With this in mind, it is important to answer the question: Who are the Cultural Creatives? In his study, "The Emerging Culture," Paul H. Ray defines their characteristics:

- Women: 60 percent; Men: 40 percent
- Median Age: 42
- Median Family Income: $47,500
- Upper Middle Class (46 percent are in the top quartile of income distribution)
- Ready to take action on their values

As consumers, Cultural Creatives make careful decisions, gather information (more from print, radio, and friends than from TV), want their purchases to reflect their values (especially large purchases such as homes), desire quality, and see the world holistically. They enjoy gathering large amounts of information and process that information to get a feel for the big picture. They want answers—Where did the product originate? Who was involved in its production? What will happen to the product when they are through using it? Telling the story of the product can compel Cultural Creatives to make a purchase decision.

Ecological sustainability is one of this group's core values. Viewing nature as sacred, they want to see an end to excessive pollution. They believe in limits to growth and in living simply. They are willing to make financial contributions to restore and protect the environment. They are optimistic and are thus unresponsive to scarcity and fear as motivators. In spite of this, offering environmentally sound products isn't enough to get Cultural Creatives to buy. For 90-95 percent of Cultural Creatives, price and quality are still the primary determinants in making a purchase.

According to an article featured in American Demographics magazine, entitled "Growing the Green Market,"[1] five environmental categories are apparent in the American population:

• **True-Blue Greens** (10 percent of the population) are proactive environmentalists. They are highly educated and have high-income levels. They are politically and socially active and are willing to pay seven percent more for environmentally sound products.

• **Greenback Greens** (5 percent of the population) are only moderately active in environmental causes, but they offer philosophical and financial support. They may pay up to 20 percent more for ecologically friendly goods and services.

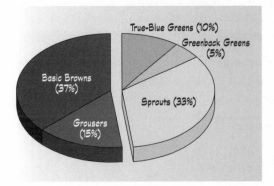

True-Blue Greens (10%)
Greenback Greens (5%)
Basic Browns (37%)
Sprouts (33%)
Grousers (15%)

• **Sprouts** (33 percent of the population) are just beginning to adopt environmental behaviors and are willing to pay 4 percent more for green products.

• The final two groups, **Grousers** (15 percent) and **Basic Browns** (37 percent), are unlikely to pay any increased amount for environmental products. Grousers believe in environmental causes but don't feel they have the time or resources to take action. In addition, Grousers believe that environmental responsibility falls on the shoulders of the company rather than on the consumer. Browns don't channel any thought or energy into ecological concerns.

This research shows that almost 50 percent of your market is open to and interested in green building. It reinforces the numbers of Cultural Creatives. Targeting these groups gives you wide latitude in market demographics and also tends to include the segment of the market most able to buy your homes.

Other research identifies a similar cultural shift away from the Dominant Social Paradigm[2] (belief system). The Dominant Social Paradigm entails a belief in limitless resources, continuous progress, and the necessity of growth. This group also has faith that science and technology can solve pressing problems. Yet, a competing set of beliefs, called the New Environmental Paradigm, is rapidly emerging. Here the focus is on restricting growth, protecting the integrity of ecosystems, and living in harmony with nature. The New Environmental Paradigm was born out of Americans' concerns about the environment. For instance:

• 79 percent consider themselves environmentalists.
• 82 percent have recycled.
• 83 percent have changed shopping habits to help protect the environment.
• 67 percent would be willing to pay 5-10 percent more for environmentally friendly products. [3]

Another major study by The Harwood Group[4] reveals that the majority of Americans see the following problems as endangering our country's future: greed and selfishness, increased stress on families and communities, and the deteriorating environment (86 percent).

All three social studies suggest that individuals with greater environmental concern are likely to engage in ecologically conscious consumer behavior (ECCB). Cultural Creatives are especially interested in new kinds of products and services. Therefore, a large potential market exists for green homes.

——— Environmentally Conscious ——— Consumer Behavior and Home Buying

The Denver HBA survey and a survey conducted by a Boulder, Colorado production builder show consumer behavior in purchasing a home. The information is insightful and relevant to green building awareness and the effectiveness of marketing—two issues that must be addressed to ensure the prosperity of green building.

Importance of Green Features to Denver Homebuyers

Survey Used
Denver HBA Built Green Consumer Awareness Survey. Survey composition: 626 recent homebuyers (1997-1998) in Denver, Colorado metro area.

The Denver Homebuilders Association's Built Green program is a new residential construction certification program. The program spent more than $600,000 in public relations and marketing over two-and-a-half years of operations. This survey was conducted to evaluate the effectiveness of marketing and the awareness level of new Built Green homebuyers.

This study gave builders perspective on their local marketing efforts. Green building categories related to home purchasing decisions were surveyed. Sixty-five percent of homeowners surveyed purchased homes under $200,000—30 percent of them purchased homes between $150,000 and $200,000; and the other 35 percent purchased homes under $150,000.

Question: Please rank on a scale of 1 to 5, how important the following factors are to you. (Measures environmental concern)

Those who had heard of Built Green:

Area of Interest	% who chose 5 or 4
Energy efficiency	89%
Water efficiency	85%
Healthy indoor air	84.5%
Preservation of natural resources	73%
Recycled content materials	46%

Of the 626 participants, in only two years, 121 (19 percent) had heard of the Built Green Program, and most of these were in their 30s. The level of environmental concern of those who had heard of Built Green is shown below. By placing a high level of importance on environmental features in a home, buyers who knew of Built Green said that they used this knowledge in their buying decisions.

This survey shows the rapid rate of market penetration of green building awareness. Buyers find the features important enough to impact their buying decision.

The Relative Value of Environmental Features to Traditional Purchase Decisions

> **Survey Used**
>
> *"Boulder, Colorado Production Builder" Environmental Development Survey*, 1997.

In a post-occupancy survey conducted by McStain Enterprises of Boulder, Colorado, a major production builder and founding member of the Built Green program, an interesting buyer profile emerged. McStain promotes green features extensively to prospective homebuyers to differentiate its homes from other builders' homes in a highly competitive environment. This survey contrasts buyers' reasons for purchasing a home in a green subdivision with the same models built several miles away that did not include the green features.

The conclusion from this study is that with other variables kept equal, **the environmental package was as important to the educated buyer as quality and price of the homes**, second only to location in importance. As a result of this study, McStain now builds all its homes with the environmental package. The bottom line is that awareness of green building features can be a significant factor in homebuyers' purchase decisions. This study has positive implications for developers and builders who market the advantages of green building in their sales programs.

Reason for Purchase	Green Subdivision	Conventional Subdivision
Location	72%	74%
Construction quality	47%	46%
Value/Price	47%	36%
Floor plan	44%	56%
Size	38%	46%
Builder reputation	41%	44%
Neighborhood	44%	38%
Environmental Package	47%	8%

Change in Consumer Values Resulting From Green Marketing

> **Survey Used**
>
> *The Genesis Group*, Denver, Colorado

The Genesis Group study targeted new homebuyers in the Denver area. The results of this survey reveal that issues addressed by green building (energy efficiency, indoor air quality, and sustainable resource use) are important to homebuyers.

With more than half to three-fourths of the general population rating green home features as very important, it is clear that green building can potentially become the mainstream approach to doing construction.

Percentage of recent home buyers who rated the given environmental feature as "important" or "very important."

Feature	Have heard of Built Green Program	Have not heard
Energy efficiency	83%	72%
Water efficiency	78%	71%
Healthy indoor air	83%	70%
Preservation of natural resources	68%	55%

——— Target Audience Surveys ———

These surveys address the innovators of green building as identified through AIA and Environmental Design & Construction surveys. Primarily architects, respondents answered questions about the green building industry. AIA Committee on the Environment readership surveys addressed the following areas: integrating green building materials and practices in current projects, perception of the value of building green, and expected growth of green building.

Client's Interest in Environmentally Considerate Building and Design, as Perceived by Architects

> **Survey Used**
>
> *American Institute of Architects COTE Survey*, 1998, 37 respondents, all architects.

Respondents were asked to rate their clients' interest level in environmental design and construction. Responses to the survey indicate that clients' level of interest in some aspects of environmentally considerate design and construction is lower than that of the architects. But when their self-interest is involved, such as with energy efficiency and indoor air quality, the clients express

Question: How important are these environmental issues to your clients?
(Participants ranked interest areas as follows: 1 = lowest interest, 5 = high importance.)

Area of interest	Mean	% who chose 5 or 4
Energy efficiency	4.27	81%
Indoor air quality	4.12	83%
Resource conservation	3.52	47%
Water conservation	3.38	42%
Land use issues	3.29	43%
Transportation efficiency	3.1	40%

high interest. This small sample and other anecdotal data suggest that architects are increasingly designing green buildings and providing leadership in the marketplace.

Architects & Building Professional Interest in Environmental Design and Construction

Surveys Used

1. *American Institute of Architects Member Survey*, Professional Interest Area Membership Profile, 1997-1998, 45 respondents.

2. *Environmental Design and Construction Publication Feasibility Study*, 1997, 570 respondents. The survey consisted of approximately 45-50% architects, the balance made up of building owners/developers and building contractors and others. Of the respondents, 333 are subscribers to *Environmental Building News* and thus have prior interest in green building; the other the remaining 237 do not necessarily have a particular interest in green building.

A mix of building professionals' (mostly architects) interest in environmental design and construction was measured in two surveys that share similar results. Areas considered are listed below in order of importance. Where questions were the same, means were averaged from both surveys. The median figure reflects the percentage of how many participants responded with a 5 or 4, which indicated strong interest. Energy efficiency and indoor air quality showed the highest interest.

Question: Rate your interest in the following areas of environmentally considerate design and construction. (Participants ranked interest areas as follows: 1=lowest interest, 5=high importance.

Area of interest	Mean	% who chose 5 or 4
Energy efficiency	4.6	95%
Indoor air quality	4.4	82%
Waste	4.1	67%
Planning and land use	3.8	62%

(AIA Member Survey)

The high level of interest in green building features among architects is important because they have significant influence on including these features in the design. Homeowners, on the other hand, despite their interest in energy efficiency and indoor air quality, only moderately influence the existence of these features in their homes. Given the consistency of interest in energy conservation and indoor air quality on the part of both architects and homeowners, it is important to consider them as top priorities in developing new green home designs.

Current Incorporation of Green Building Materials

> **Survey Used**
>
> *Environmental Design and Construction Publication Feasibility Study*, 1997, 590 respondents. The survey consisted of approximately 45-50% architects, the balance made up of building owners/developers, building contractors, and others. Of the respondents, 333 are subscribers to *Environmental Business News* and thus have prior interest in green building. The remaining 237 do not necessarily have an interest in green building.

In a study to determine whether there was a market for an Environmental Design and Construction magazine, ED&C found that 94 percent of their respondents were already incorporating aspects or elements in architectural design or construction that could be defined as environmentally considerate. Seventy-six percent of respondents felt this percentage would increase within the next year. More than 75 percent of ED&C respondents reported that 46 percent of their projects include environmentally considerate aspects.

The graph shows that 20 percent of the 521 respondents reported that over 75 percent of the building materials they use are environmentally considerate. This impressive percentage (94 percent) of architects, builders, developers, and others who are already incorporating green designs reveals that a shift has already occurred toward accepting and using environmentally friendly features.

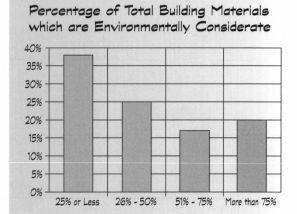

Percentage of Total Building Materials which are Environmentally Considerate

Percentage of New Construction Incorporating Green Features

Survey Used
American Institute of Architects COTE Survey, 1998, 37 respondents, all architects.

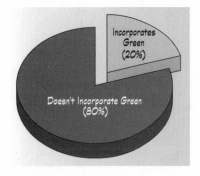

When architects were asked what percentage of new construction incorporates green features today, answers varied from .1 percent to 100 percent. The mean figure was 20.3 percent.

These architects are the self-selected members of the AIA Committee on the Environment. A 20 percent market penetration in just a few years shows a tremendous rate of growth from almost no consumer knowledge of green features only five years ago.

Future Demand for Green Building

Surveys Used
1. *American Institute of Architects COTE Survey*, 1998, 37 respondents, all architects.
2. *Environmental Design and Construction Publication Feasibility Study*, 1997, 590 respondents. The survey consisted of approximately 45-50% architects, the balance made up of building owners/developers, building contractors, and others. Of the respondents, 333 are subscribers to *Environmental Business News* and thus have prior interest in green building. The remaining 237 do not necessarily have an interest in green building.

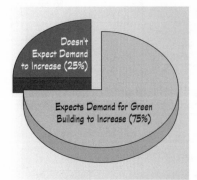

Eighty-nine percent of ED&C respondents predict that green building will increase. Seventy-five percent of AIA COTE respondents expect the demand for green building to increase in the near future.

While architects on average believe that about 20% of new construction already incorporates green features, 75 percent predict that demand will rise for green building. This information reveals that there is interest in and room for growth for green in the building industry.

Marketing Suggestions Based on Current Consumer Behavior

The surveys in this chapter highlight several points in terms of marketing green building. First, identify your target market. Are they "true-blues," "greenback greens," or "sprouts?" The more competitive your price and the more you can showcase quality, the broader your target market can be. When you market your homes emphasize the benefits to the homeowner of incorporating green features. If green homes are not as easy to purchase as conventional homes, buying behavior drops considerably, despite consumers' inclinations to buy green.

Second, make information clear and readily available. Because most consumers simply are not knowledgeable about green buildings, they might not realize they could have a green home unless you tell them what green involves and show them the benefits. Consumers are confused as they make decisions about which products are better for the environment, such as choosing paper or plastic bags at the grocery store. You have an opportunity to clarify their options and to help them make environmentally sound decisions. Again, remember that information and the whole story behind the products you use and how they improve the home are vital to Cultural Creatives. You can't give a Creative too much information about what you have built into their home and why.

Third, know your selling points. Since homeowners are most interested in indoor air quality (IAQ) and energy efficiency, information should lay out the health implications of poor IAQ and what you have done to alleviate these problems. The benefits of energy efficiency should highlight increased comfort and long term savings, supported by quantifiable data. This benefit-based sales approach also allows you to sell other features such as resource efficiency and water conservation.

Caroline Hoyt, Owner
Tom Hoyt, Owner
Kristin Shewfelt, Director of Market Research & Environmental Programs
McStain Enterprises, Inc., Boulder, CO
(303) 494-5900

McStain was founded thirty-two years ago by architectural designers, Tom and Caroline Hoyt. Since they built their environmental research house in 1994, McStain has been striving to increase the environmental sustainability of the 300-400 homes they build each year. The Hoyts and Shewfelt have all been named to the Denver Metro Built Green Hall of Fame. Additionally, McStain received seven awards in Boulder's Fall Tour of Homes (1998), including three awards for Best Use of Environmental Products.

Environmental issues and consumer concern about the environment are creating a strong market for green building. Green building translates into a quality of life improvement for many consumers. Your responsibility is to give consumers clear examples of how your homes provide them the opportunity to make the environmentally sound choices they want to make.

Tom Hoyt says, "What's going to make you the leader? We think it's this ability to meet people's needs on more than just a physical level. Purchasing a green home makes homebuyers feel like they are a part of the whole environmental movement. Not only are they saving money, they are making a decision for the long term. Three homeowners down the road may receive the benefit as well as the original owner. In every national survey you see, environmental consciousness is extremely high in the buying public. What isn't high is any sense of what exactly they can do for the environment. Green building provides the answer."

Conducting Your Own Market Research

National consumer trends can give you valuable information about how to direct your marketing. In addition, knowing the characteristics and desires of the people in your area and knowing who is a target buyer for your homes will help you focus your marketing efforts and create homes that will sell.

Collecting and analyzing data can seem less than appealing and where to start and what questions to ask can be overwhelming. This section offers you pointers on where to find research that has already been done and how to do your own market research. These pointers should make the process simpler and hopefully, even enjoyable.

From Your Desk

To get started, you don't need to leave your desk. Several valuable Internet sites provide useful data. An excellent source is the U.S. Department of Commerce Bureau of the Census Web site. At <www.census.gov>, you can find statistics on averages such as individual and household income, household size, number of children and age, among many others. The information can be broken down into areas as specific as zip codes and even individual streets. If you don't have Internet access, your can contact the Census Bureau by calling (301) 457-4100 or by faxing (301) 457-4714. Data from the 2000 census should be available by 2001.

Whereas the census is only updated every ten years, The U.S. Department of Housing and Urban Development publishes a quarterly report on housing market conditions and trends and on housing needs by region. You can access this information on the Internet at <www.huduser.org> or call (800) 483-2209.

Other useful resources for national and regional information on various topics:

- **The U.S. Department of Labor:** Employment trends, wages, occupational groups, and consumers. Web site: <http://gatekeeper.dol.gov>, Tel: (301) 202-5767
- *American Demographics* **Magazine:** Online information, magazine subscriptions, book orders, marketing tools directory. Web site: <www.marketingtools.com>.
- **The National Association of Realtors:** Information on price, size, and age of homes on the market broken down on a town-by-town-level, as well as information on quality of schools, crime levels, and cultural amenities. Web site: <www.realtors.com>.

Other places to contact include your local Chamber of Commerce, local HBA, city and county departments, public and private universities, neighborhood associations, and the state department of commerce. Your lender and title company can likely provide you with information on areas of building activity, volume of activity, and prices. Another great source is the media. Newspaper, television and radio stations all have research departments. Media researchers have extensive databases available to them. They know how to analyze the data and can often provide you with complete consumer demographics quickly.

Research that Requires Legwork

Statistics provide reliable and scientific information about your potential buyers, but personal contact with people in your buyer profile can give you a better sense of what your buyers want. In addition, individual contact gives you the opportunity to ask specific questions and to understand the reasoning that underlies people's choices.

Visit neighborhoods that are either near to where you are building or similar to the kind of neighborhoods in which you are building. Start by simply taking an audit of the neighborhood: How many one- and two-story houses are there? What kinds of cars are parked in the driveways? Is the neighborhood lively during the day or deserted by commuters? Are the lawns and exteriors of the houses well maintained? What evidence is there of kids in the neighborhood?

While you are there, knock on a few doors. Ask residents questions. Weekends are generally a good time to find people at home.

Colleen Edwards, president of a San Francisco advertising firm and author of From Good Market Research to Great Marketing *(Home Builder Press), suggests asking some of the following questions:*

- *What do you like best about your home? Why?*
- *What would you change in your home? Why?*
- *What rooms do you use most? Would you change their design or size in any way?*
- *Did you modify your home with any options or upgrades? How satisfied are you with them?*
- *How do you use your front yard? Your backyard? How would you change one or the other if you could?*
- *If you could make one room in your home bigger, even at the expense of making another room smaller or losing it completely, which would it be?*
- *Which would you modify to gain that space? Why?*
- *Where do you or your spouse commute? How long does it take?*
- *Where do you shop?*
- *If you have children, are they in public school? How satisfied are you with the school(s)?*
- *If you were going to give me one piece of advice about building new homes in this area, what would it be?*

Since you are focusing specifically on marketing the green components of your homes, ask questions relating to these features such as:

- Are there many energy efficient features in your home?
- Were any of your appliances chosen for their water or energy conserving features?
- On average, what do you pay per month for energy?
- Do you know if any of the paint, cabinetry, carpet, etc. in your house was chosen to protect indoor air quality?
- Which environmental features of a home are most important to you: the level of indoor air quality, the level of energy efficiency, or the conservation of resources used in building it?
- Have you added any environmental features to your home since you bought it? Which features?

➡ Another possibility for gathering input from homeowners and potential buyers is to host an information social. This kind of an event is easy to put on and can give you a valuable opportunity to receive feedback on the homes you are planning. Simply announce the event and its purpose, either through an ad in the local paper, calling some of your contacts, or sending out a direct mailing. Ask for people to make reservations. Hold the event in a community gathering place such as the local civic center and provide beverages, hors d'oeuvres, or dessert. Display drawings of the neighborhood, individual homes, floor plans, and information about the environmental features and their benefits.

An information social provides a relaxed atmosphere for you and your staff to discuss your homes with people who are interested in green building. It is also an opportunity for you to both sell your homes and to get good ideas from potential buyers.

There are many other places and ways to get a feel for the green market. Be creative. Maybe host an interior decorating class in one of your model homes. Not only will this bring people into your homes, it might also get them thinking about what they could do stylistically in a new home that they can't do in their current residence. Think about other industries that are targeting the same type of consumer you are. What approach are they taking in their market research and advertis-  ing? Understanding who your buyers will be and what they want is powerful information. That knowledge will give you the ability to build homes that will not only sell, but make your customers happy over the long term.

Tom Hoyt, of McStain Enterprises says, "We have in our mission statement—'Design and build visionary communities that integrate the aesthetic, physical and emotional needs of our customers.' Traditionally, we were focused on the physical needs, which you can determine through conventional market research. You can find out what size a kitchen needs to be in today's world and what pieces it needs to have in it to satisfy peoples needs if they are busy working or if they are staying at home. What is much harder to do is to understand what the deep seeded emotional and aesthetic needs are. We draw a parallel with a piece of art or a great piece of music. The customer doesn't tell the artist that they want a certain line weight or particular colors, and then expect to come up with a great piece of art. They rely on an artist to create that. You have to understand how a piece of art pulls all those elements together, which makes the difference between a bunch of colors and lines and a real piece of art. Doing this with homes is the professional responsibility of the builder and designer."

Conclusion

Clearly there is a market just waiting for green building. As the research in this chapter reveals, a strong segment of the population is ready to buy environmentally sound products. And, for those who are well informed about the benefits of green building, the environmental package included with their home is second only to location in their purchasing decision. Builders and architects alike believe that green building will corner increasing amounts of the market share for new home construction.

Chapter 2 will look into the environmental issues that create a place and a future for green building.

Endnotes

1. Speer, Tibbett, L., "Growing the Green Market," *American Demographics,* August 1997. <www.demographics.com/Publications/AD/97_ad/9708_ad/AD97082.htm>

2. *Dominant Social Paradigm* (Catton and Dunlap, 1978, 1980; Dunlap and Van Liere, 1978). This paradigm entails: 1) Belief in limitless resources, continuous progress, and the necessity of growth; 2) Faith in the problem-solving abilities of science and technology; 3) Strong emotional commitment to a laissez-faire economy and to the sanctity of private property rights.

3. *Dominant Social Paradigm*, Catton and Dunlap, 1978, 1980; Dunlap and Van Liere, 1978.

4. Harwood group survey footnote

What is Green Building?

2

This chapter discusses processes and materials involved in green building. It also offers pros and cons regarding green alternatives in the context of conventional construction.

Environmental Issues that Create the Market for Green Buildings - The green building market in its simplest form is based on four overarching categories: energy efficiency, indoor air quality, resource conservation, and water use.

The Effect of Building Green on the Construction Process - Green building starts from the beginning. More than just a building process, it is a thinking process. Site planning, design, construction, and materials must be reconsidered from a green perspective.

What is Green Building? There are as many ways to build green as there are builders in this country. There are also many "shades" of green. The darker green it is, the more environmentally friendly or sustainable the house is. This chapter discusses the environmental aspects of conventional construction and how green substitutions can reduce some of the impacts traditionally associated with building new buildings. However, these technical considerations are for your eyes primarily. The information in this chapter can help you in your decision-making process on how to start building green. Your customers want to hear a different story. How to sell what you have built will be discussed in Chapters 5 and 6.

"What's the use of a house if you haven't got a tolerable planet to put it on?"

—Henry David Thoreau, 1845

Environmental Issues That Create the Market for Green Buildings

Your customer is being bombarded with environmental information on a daily basis. The issues covered in this chapter are not to convince you that your customer is right or wrong. It is intended to provide a basis for communication about issues of increasing importance to your prospective buyers. Considering the controversy of many environmental issues, there are few areas where the data is black and white. But if the customer is always right, it is important to know what they are thinking in order to sell them the green features of your house.

Primary Features of Green Buildings

- *Energy Efficiency*
- *Indoor Air Quality*
- *Resource Conservation*
- *Water Use*

Because green building is relatively new in the market place, many mainstream builders are not even aware of the many alternatives that this approach to construction provides. Just as the energy crisis of the late '70s created a market for innovative energy conserving products, the following environmental issues are creating the market for green homes.

——— Energy Efficiency ———

Reducing Dependence on Oil

Energy efficiency is just applied common sense: The more we use, the less we have for future generations. Many Americans believe that we have become complacent about the low cost of energy and that the days of cheap energy could be running out. According to oil analysts Colin Campbell and Jean Laherrère's article in *Scientific American*, known petroleum reserves will be in decline by 2010-2020.[1] As these reserves decline, oil becomes more difficult and more expensive to tap. In addition, the energy we use for electricity and heating adds to the clouds of pollution over our major cities. Because of extraction costs and air quality concerns, oil will eventually become too expensive to burn for heat or electricity. In addition, as oil costs rise, so do the prices of other energy sources.

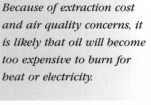

Because of extraction cost and air quality concerns, it is likely that oil will become too expensive to burn for heat or electricity.

Reducing Energy Consumption

Green building reduces energy consumption in numerous ways. First, we can decrease the energy embodied in the materials themselves through efficient design, use of recycled and local materials, and recycling construction waste. Second, green building design reduces a building's energy consumption over its lifetime. Strategically placing windows and skylights can eliminate the need for electrical lighting during the day. A whole-house fan can cool the house overnight, rather than relying on air conditioning. High quality insulation reduces temperature regulation costs in both summer and winter.

Incorporating Solar Energy

Houses can easily increase their use of passive heating and cooling. South facing windows with overhangs can reduce heating costs by 20 to 30 percent, and prevailing breezes, shading, and natural plantings can keep houses cool in the summer.

Incorporating passive design, solar hot water heating, or photovoltaics (solar electric systems) into a home is a prudent

investment for you and your customer. This list only scratches the surface of the possibilities for reducing a building's energy requirements.

—— Indoor Air Quality ——

Indoor air quality is a quiet crisis that is only now reaching the public's attention. Dust, pollen, smoke and airborne chemicals all contribute to the degradation of air quality. As the energy efficiency of homes has increased, the issue has become more acute because the air in homes is exchanged less often with outside air.

The Environmental Protection Agency has been researching the problem for over a decade and has found that indoor pollutants may be a significant factor in the health of home occupants. As sited in "The Environmental Life-cycle Analysis of Floor Coverings" indoor air in homes with low infiltration rates can lead to environmental sensitivity or health problems in as many as 15 percent of the public.[2] The *New England Journal of Medicine* in a report to the Massachusetts legislature has stated that up to 40 percent of children born today may develop respiratory problems.[3]

As the evidence mounts, your customers will hear more about the negative effects of products and chemicals used inside the home. Many will become concerned about their health and the health of their children. As a builder, you should be prepared for the customers who will require more careful attention.

Indoor Pollutants

Modern buildings can contain airborne particulates, volatile organic compounds (VOCs), formaldehyde, mold, and fungi. In fact, the same air pollutants covered by environmental laws outdoors can often be found at much higher levels in the average American residence. Of the hundreds of air pollutants covered under existing U.S. laws, only ozone and sulfur dioxide remain more prevalent outdoors.[4] These laws have generally focused more on the sources of the pollution than on the greatest amount of exposure to pollutants. Our homes emit relatively small amounts of pollution, and yet they are often the places where we face the greatest exposure to health-threatening pollutants.

40% of children born today will develop respiratory disease in part due to the chemicals in their homes.

For instance, in the February 1998 issue of *Scientific American*, authors Wayne Ott and John Roberts state that indoor air contains at least five (but typically 10 or more) times higher concentrations of pesticides than outside air. The authors cite another study that reports, "in more than half the households surveyed, the concentrations of seven toxic organic chemicals . . . were above the levels that would trigger a formal risk assessment for residential soil at a Superfund site."[5]

Many products are manufactured with formaldehyde, which has been identified by the EPA and the New York University Medical Center as a possible human carcinogen.[6] Cabinets, counter tops, shelving, and furniture are made from particleboard that is glued together with formaldehyde. This chemical can be released (or out-gassed) into the home for years. Paints and floor finishes also contain chemicals such as benzene compounds and crosslinkers that are unhealthy to breathe. That "new house smell" is actually the odor of volatile organic compounds (VOCs) and is a telltale sign that harmful chemicals exist in the indoor environment.

One Family's Nightmare

One day I got a call from a homeowner who was at his wit's end. He recounted that for several months his kids had been constantly sick with headaches, fever, coughs, and other flu-like symptoms. The doctors didn't seem to be able to help the kids, who were missing a lot of school. During the same period, his wife had two or three migraine headaches a week. She was losing a lot of sleep. All of them were exasperated.

He asked me if these conditions could possibly be from something in his home. I asked him many questions about their home and lifestyle. I asked if they had done any remodeling. Nothing seemed relevant to their situation.

Finally, he told me he had gotten a bonus at work and had bought built-in shelves and desks for his kids and their master bedroom. He hadn't mentioned it because he couldn't see how that made any difference. I asked him to go to the rooms and pull out a shelf and describe to me what he saw. It turned out to be particleboard with a melamine veneer.

I suggested that he try an experiment. Take everything off the shelves and remove them for the weekend since all the shelf edges were unfinished and the particleboard was exposed. I asked him to call me a week later to report if there was any difference. He called and said that the kids' symptoms had decreased and he was encouraged. The next weekend he removed all of the built-in cabinetry. He called me two weeks later and said all of their symptoms were gone. The kids felt great and his wife hadn't had a headache since he took the shelves out.

Reducing Pollution

Product manufacturers in the construction industry have monitored the increase of these indoor air pollutants and have developed alternate products to remedy indoor toxicity. For example, solvent-free adhesives eliminate many suspected and known human carcinogens, and they often adhere better than conventional adhesives. Paints free of VOCs are now available. Some new engineered wood products use adhesives that contain no formaldehyde.

For customers who are concerned about this issue, green buildings can reduce potential IAQ problems through a number of alternatives: providing good ventilation to allow fresh air to flow through the house; installing an exhaust system for radon gas; avoiding wood products that contain formaldehyde and sealing those which do; and using low- or no-VOC interior paint, solvent-free finishes, and solvent-free construction adhesives.

——— Resource Conservation ———

A variety of market forces have affected the construction industry and resulted in an increased interest in green building alternatives. One such force is the depletion of natural resources, which has given rise to resource-efficient building. In addition to consuming large amounts of energy, commercial and residential buildings account for roughly 40 percent of the materials entering the global economy each year.[7] Approximately three billion tons of raw materials are turned into foundations, walls, pipes, and panels. Quarrying earth and rock to create bricks, gravel, sand, and blocks leaves large scars in the landscape. Other building materials such as aluminum, steel, and plastic require even heavier processing.

Wood Use

According to the World Resources Institute, America has harvested over 95 percent of its old-growth forests,[8] which has increased the pressure on the forest products industry to develop substitutes for conventional lumber. The building industry accounts for almost half of the world's demand for wood. Of that, one-third goes into lumber, plywood, particleboard, and other structural building material.[9]

Worldwide consumption of industrial timber (approximately 1.66 billion tons per year) exceeds the use of steel and plastics combined.[10] The results of this high rate of timber consumption are the loss of the world's forests at a rate of 37 million acres a year (approximately half the land area of Finland). The average house requires harvesting an acre of trees.[11]

Our forests are not just declining in area, but also in quality. Twenty years ago, the average old-growth tree harvested from national forests was 24" in diameter. Today the average is 13". This shows up on the job site as lower quality lumber with more knots, unusable twisted boards, and boards that warp once they are in place.

Old-growth forest: A forest in which at least some trees are more than 200 years old

Engineered Lumber and Recycled Materials

Engineered lumber products are an innovative alternative to solid-sawn lumber materials. Forest products companies have developed engineered lumber products to utilize fast-growing farm trees. These products are stronger, straighter, and lighter, and may use only 50 percent of the wood fiber to perform the same structural functions as solid-sawn lumber. Fast-growing tree farms, where forest product companies are planting more trees today than they harvest, are an example of a sustainable resource.

Strategic use of recycled content building materials has grown out of the increasing stockpiles of recycled material. Americans are recycling seven times more than they did a decade ago. Building materials are a perfect application for recycled refuse. Not only does recycling divert waste from landfills, but many of the remanufactured materials are of higher quality and durability than conventional materials. We can easily incorporate many resource-efficient materials, reclaimed wood, and recycled-content products such as carpet, decking, cellulose, and fiberglass insulation into homes cost-effectively.

——— Water Use ———

The Gold of the Twenty-First Century

Water will be the gold of the twenty-first century in many parts of the country. In the twentieth century, human water use increased at twice the rate of population growth.[12] Today domestic water use accounts for 8 percent of the world's fresh water consumption. The population on the planet is expected to double in the next twenty-five years, causing water supplies to be stressed.

Water Consumption

The amount of water we use in our daily lives can be surprising. Showering, on average, uses five gallons of water per minute. Flushing our toilets uses four to five gallons of drinking-quality water per flush with older toilets, and 1.6 gallons with newer toilets. Watering the lawn uses about 11 gallons of potable water per minute. Although domestic use only accounts for a small fraction of total water use, rapid urban growth has resulted in depleted groundwater sources in Los Angeles, San Diego, and Tucson, and other cities across the country, forcing these areas to take water from far-reaching places.

Additionally, some construction materials require large quantities of water to produce: one pound of steel requires 32 gallons of water, and one pound of aluminum requires 1,000 gallons of water.[13]

Reducing Water Consumption

With minimal impact on our current lifestyles, we can reduce our domestic water use by as much as half. Many options such as water-conserving faucets, toilets, and dishwashers are available that will help preserve this important resource if they are widely implemented.

The Effect of Building Green on the Construction Process

The Beginning of My Green Building Career

My construction company was hired to build a large addition for a family about fifteen years ago. At first they seemed like the perfect client. They had come from New England to Washington, D.C., and were very energy conscious. They wanted a home that would last for at least a hundred years like the old colonial they had moved from.

We discussed opening the view to the south overlooking a valley and wooded forest. Lots of sunlight and views appealed to them as long as it wouldn't be too hot in the D.C. summer heat. Planning was going like a dream.

Once we had the exterior designed and started to move inside, they dropped a bombshell. They told us their son was allergic to everything: grass, dust, mold, pollen, perfumes, and most building materials! We must have had a look that displayed our horror at the thought of the nightmare ahead because they laughed and said, "Well, perhaps not all building materials."

I was a typical builder. I wanted finishes that would last as long as the shell. I used "Swedish" floor finishes, oil based paint, and solvent-based trim stain. We always installed fiberglass insulation as thick as we could fit it in. Wood paneling was a given in the library. To ensure that everything stayed in place, we screwed and glued the house together.

This was my first exposure to the whole concept of indoor air quality and the health impacts of building materials. I had no idea that so many of the products we used were toxic to someone who is sensitive to their living environment.

We went into an intense research mode. This was fifteen years ago, when there was little information on toxicology of building materials and there were very few products on the market that were geared toward healthy indoor air quality. To find out what the boy would react to, we had him sleep with products near his bed. We found out that particleboard was an irritant and caused him to dive onto his respirator. We were clueless about why it was a problem, but we ruled it out along with the walnut paneling and the MDF trim. We discovered that oil-based paint, latex paint, and wood finishes were also not acceptable. It took us a long time to find a paint company that made "organic" paint that we could use.

One product at a time we were able to find substitutes that he could live with. The project went way over budget due to the specialties we had to incorporate, and our profit margin was reduced because it took so long to find the products. We figured that you pay for your education one way or another and felt like we had learned a lot in the process.

Today there are resources that make the whole process much easier. Manufacturers of almost any product type imaginable have developed green substitutes, many of which cost about the same as conventional products. (See Chapter 3.) The design community has developed good methodologies and sources for designing green buildings.

Green Building Step-by-Step

Green buildings reduce the impact of the built environment on the ecosystem and the health of occupants through careful design, specification, construction, operation, and reuse or deconstruction at the end of a building's useful life.

Building green calls for new considerations in each step of the design and construction process. The rest of this chapter explores conventional approaches and a sampling of green alternatives that address the environmental issues raised by common construction approaches.

Each of the following sections provides perspectives and offers considerations on how to incorporate green in your design and construction process.

Stages of Construction Affected by Building Green:

- *Site Planning*
- *Design*
- *Construction Process*
- *Materials/Specifications*
- *Foundations*
- *Structural/Framing*
- *Sheathing/Exterior Finish*
- *Insulation*
- *Roofing*
- *Doors and Windows*
- *Flooring/Floor Covering*
- *Paints/Coatings/Adhesives*
- *Exterior Finish/Trim*

——— Site Planning ———

Tom Hoyt, president of McStain Enterprises, says, "I keep looking at the green planning side of things from the standpoint of a well-planned neighborhood. In the typical market place today, twice as many consumers buy an existing home than a new home. Why is that? To a large extent it is the character of neighborhoods. You are able to look at an established neighborhood and know whether it is successful or not, whether it is located right or not. In a new community it is much harder to make that determination without experience. So we've kept existing neighborhoods as our model."

Hoyt says he wants to create the kind of neighborhood diversity that includes a variety of housing types and price ranges so that grandma can live next door or a college kid down the street can watch neighbors' kids at night. Development planning that uses new urbanism approaches such as putting the garage in the back and a porch on the front are becoming increasingly popular. To reinstate a sense of traditional community in new neighborhoods, these developers are abandoning cul-de-sacs and are creating friendlier streetscapes, for example, by narrowing the streets and planting trees between the curb and the detached sidewalk.

Green Building is a Thinking Process

Green building is more than a building process; it is a thinking process. When you have the opportunity to develop a site for a new neighborhood, consider things that can enhance the green aspects of the homes. Before the backhoe arrives on site, take the following considerations into account:

- How does the house sit on the lot?
- Has the site been predetermined by the developer or by setback limits?

- How does the house relate to the site?
- Can old trees be preserved?
- Can interesting features such as large stones, swales, or natural growth be preserved and enhanced?
- Are there wildlife habitats that can be protected?
- What are the natural water flows through the property?
- Can they be enhanced for storm water runoff?
- How will the occupants use the lot?
- Is outdoor space designed into the project?
- Are south and east orientations protected to extend the seasons when they can be used?
- From which directions do prevailing breezes come? Window designs can be oriented to take advantage of breezes and enhance comfort.

One Green Building Challenge

On one project, the builder challenged me to take an existing model home that he had built dozens of times and make it "green." This was an opportunity for many reasons, but the most problematic aspect was dealing with site issues.

The house was designed to take advantage of western views, so the west wall had a large expanse of glass. I worked with the builder to find a site that would allow what had been the west elevation to face south. I ran computer calculations on the impact of changing the glass from the west to the south side. The west glass orientation required air conditioning because of afternoon heat gain in the summer. The south orientation would not. The south orientation also reduced the heating load in the winter by increasing the passive solar gain.

The total savings on energy bills from just turning the house ninety degrees were over 30 percent.

———— Design Process ————

The greatest green changes for the lowest cost are made early, during the design process. By incorporating all the relevant design professionals into the process and making green substitutions during the design phase, you can save money in some areas and apply it to other features. Rotating the plan to the south in the example I just cited is an example of saving operating costs.

Thinking through the whole system during the design process can reduce first costs. For example, in northern climates, shallow frost-protected foundations can save money from the start. Even in deep frost zones with footers typically at 48", shallow foundations at 20" depth save on excavation, forming, and concrete costs. This can save as much as two to three thousand dollars. Designs that include finished basements can use permanent rigid foam forms to accomplish two things: savings on interior finish costs and better insulated basements.

The design process is when the greatest impacts for the lowest cost can be made.

You can save money in framing as well. By using optimum value engineering (OVE) framing, material costs can be reduced by as much as 15 percent while providing a better insulated home. When you design green, from both construction costs and sales potential, you can fuel the marketing fires. And when you can prove lower utility bills through quality construction, you win both ways. (See Chapter 4 for more details.)

——— Trade Contractors and ——— the Construction Process

Trade contractors can make or break a project, but it can be difficult to find framing crews that are willing to change the way they build. The industry, however, is changing all the time, and finding progressive trade contractors or training existing ones on how to build with new materials in new ways produces long-term benefits.

They say the devil is in the details, and this is ever so true with construction. For example, poor framing compromises homeowners' comfort and energy efficiency by creating opportunities for drafts. The plain truth is that all the best plans for a green home are dependent on your trade contractors being part of the program. (See Chapter 4.)

Missing a Detail

I was working on a house for a chemically sensitive client. The architect was committed to creating a home that was as free as possible of solvent-based products because the client was particularly sensitive to petrochemical odors.

Before the project began, I conducted a training session for the builder's staff, trade contractors, and field personnel. It was the first time all the groups had been in the same room. They enjoyed meeting each other and discussing other jobs they had worked on. We found out

All the best plans for a green home are entirely dependent on the subs being a part of the program.

later that this meeting facilitated communication between them. The training also made them feel that this job was important and that they had a significant role to play. The quality of their work improved because of the added attention they gave to the project. They also put their best workers on the job so they could learn some of the new processes. These trade contractors got a marketing niche that resulted in new business for them.

The down side was that the project took longer than projected, and the client started putting pressure on the builder to finish. In an effort to speed up the process, the superintendent brought in a new trim crew that was willing to work over the weekend. None of us knew he was doing this. We found out on Monday morning that a new crew had been working all weekend. To our chagrin, however, they had used conventional construction adhesive for all the trim. The house reeked of chemicals. Occupancy was pushed back by almost two months waiting for the chemical smell to evaporate.

The moral of the story is that even though we tried to communicate effectively with all the trade contractors, one change affected the end result of the whole project.

——— Materials/Specifications ———

The following section provides deeper understanding of the environmental impacts of standard construction and how green products create benefits. Each aspect of green building, from foundations to finishes, involves specific environmental issues.

The choice of green material selection requires many considerations that have to be driven by good business sense. It should be a gradual process. It doesn't serve you, your customers, or the planet if you go whole-hog building green from the start. That approach can have a serious negative impact on your bottom line. The question will always be how much can you afford to do? How many substitutions can you incorporate and still stay in your market niche? And how many changes can you make to ensure that when your children grow up they will have the same options of clean water, pure air, and deep forests you do?

Chapter 6 provides more specific information about green building features and benefits. At this point, however, it is important to take a look at the environmental issues concerning the materials used at each stage of the construction process.

Foundations

Concrete is technically a non-renewable resource, yet its component materials, stone, sand, and cement are abundant. Nevertheless, concrete, though highly durable, is extremely energy-intensive to produce and can cause high levels of air pollution. Concrete production is responsible for 8 percent of carbon dioxide production in the U.S.[14] There are three aspects to concrete use: strategic placement, admixture components, and forming.

Strategic placement is using concrete where it is most important. For example, shallow frost-protected foundation systems are being used with success and code approval in cold northern climates like Fargo, North Dakota. There the frost line depth is 48", and shallow foundations are only poured 20" deep. It was pointed out earlier in this chapter that significant savings can be achieved by reducing the depth of the excavation and the yards of concrete poured.

Admixture components such as calcium chloride as an accelerator, gypsum as a retarder, and sulfonated melamine formaldehyde (SMF), a potential toxin, as a plasticizer, affect the environmental impact of the concrete. The impact may be on-site or at the plant, depending on the chemical. At the same time, some admixtures may be environmentally beneficial and enhance the concrete as well. For instance, fly ash (a by-product from burning coal in power plants) added to the mixture strengthens the concrete, reduces the amount of cement required, and recycles waste from industrial and utility waste-streams.[15]

Forming concrete can account for 15-35 percent of the total cost of concrete installations. Plywood has been the mainstay of concrete forming companies for many years. With plywood, the foundation essentially gets built twice, once in wood and again in concrete. To save on wood costs, some companies have invested in reusable aluminum forms. This is a more resource-efficient solution, yet it adds labor in building and dismantling forms. Reusable forms require form-release agents. Most of these agents are petro-chemical-based and off-gas large amounts of volatile organic compounds. However, nontoxic vegetable-based form-release oils are available.

Currently, several alternatives to conventional concrete foundations use polystyrene foam boards to form walls. These come in a variety of shapes and sizes. The forms stay in place and serve as insulation for the foundation. Some foam products are treated with integral borate to deter damaging insects. Additionally, pre-cast concrete foundation walls are available in some areas. The advantages of pre-cast foundations are that they require less concrete than foundations which are site-cast, and they are designed to accommodate interior insulation.

Non-asphalt-based damp proofing reduces the risk of leaching chemicals into local aquifers and can last longer than conventional damp proofing. In some parts of the country, rigid mineral wool panels are available which help insulate foundation walls and provide effective drainage. Mineral wool typically includes iron-ore-slag (a postindustrial waste product). Recycled aggregate or crushed glass can be specified for use in the concrete or as backfill for foundation drains. To eliminate the need for periodic applications of pesticides, foundations can be designed with termite shields or back-filled with special termite-proof sand.

Structural/Framing

Wood is the most commonly used framing material. Large dimension lumber (2x10 and larger) is often milled from old-growth trees for economical harvesting and processing. However, old-growth trees as defined in this book are becoming more scarce and harder to access. Engineered lumber is now cost competitive for most applications. I-joists, oriented strand board (OSB), laminated veneer lumber (LVL), and trusses can substitute for dimensional lumber. Finger-jointed lumber in 2x4 or 2x6 studs is effective because it uses shorter pieces of wood that might otherwise have become waste and makes straighter lumber that is less likely to warp.

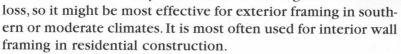

Light gauge steel framing can be used as a piece-for-piece substitute for wood, but it is not necessarily more environmentally friendly. Steel does contain some recycled content, but the light gauge steel used for framing generally has a lower recycled content than heavier steels. And all steel is energy-intensive to produce. Of even more concern is that steel is highly conductive, which may contribute to heat gain or loss, so it might be most effective for exterior framing in southern or moderate climates. It is most often used for interior wall framing in residential construction.

Masonry construction using hollow-core block masonry units (CMU) is difficult to insulate well. Autoclaved aerated concrete (AAC), a special kind of lightweight cement block, insulates better. With other types of block it is important to add insulation between the concrete block and the exterior finish.

Structural insulated panels (SIPs) are another wall framing alternative. These panels are usually made with OSB skins and foam insulation. They provide good insulation, are quite airtight, and go up quickly. Some panels substitute compressed straw for plastic foam as the core. Although these panels use straw that would otherwise go to waste, they do not provide the same degree of insulation as the foam-filled panels. Foam-core panels can also be used to fill in between post-and-beam or timber-frame structures. These heavy timber structures require large amounts of wood, but they tend to be quite durable. One way to conserve wood is to cut the post and beam timbers from demolished buildings.

Adobe, rammed-earth, straw bale and other less standard structural systems can be effective with good engineering and appropriate code approvals. Log homes, though, not only use excessive amounts of wood, but they do not insulate very well.

Sheathing/Exterior Finish

Sheathing, a secondary weather barrier behind the exterior finish, may serve as the primary substrate for attaching the finish layer and also provide diagonal bracing (rack resistance) for the structure. The exterior finish is the most visible material of the house and also the primary weather barrier. Relying on exterior finish as your only weather barrier can be risky, especially in regions with wind-driven rain or poor drying conditions. Wind and moisture will find their way into the smallest opening. Because of this, siding or exterior wall systems designed around the rain-screen principle are much more effective and durable. Such a strategy requires a vented exterior finish and a well-sealed secondary layer. Together, these layers work to balance the pressure on either side of the exterior finish, thus taking away the force that would otherwise drive moisture inwards or cause rot.

Plywood and oriented strand board (OSB) are the most common sheathing materials for residential structures. OSB, which is made from fast-growing trees of relatively low commercial value, uses a higher percentage of the tree. Plywood, on the other hand, needs larger diameter, often old growth trees to peel veneers efficiently. OSB uses a variety of sources for cellulose fiber and can incorporate various adhesive types that have different degrees of toxicity. Most OSB and plywood use phenol-formaldehyde adhesive that is less toxic than urea-formaldehyde, which is used in interior particleboard and some paneling. An OSB that uses non-formaldehyde MDI resin base for its adhesive is preferable.

Recycled content sheathing is also available. One option is a "sandwich" material using aluminum foil surface facings over a recycled wood fiber core. This sheathing meets most wind load requirements and costs less than OSB. Exterior gypsum sheathing, generally made with recycled newspaper, is an especially good option for stucco finishes

Redwood applied to the exterior is controversial in several ways. Clear heart redwood is generally cut from old-growth forests and

therefore needs to be avoided. Some second-growth lumber is available; however, it is less resistant to rot and insects than heartwood. Sustainably harvested redwood is now available that protects the old redwood forests and provides high-quality material for a small increase in price.

For deck applications, pressure-treated wood has potential health consequences to installers and inhabitants because of the chromium and arsenic in CCA (copper chromium arsenate). Both copper and arsenic are toxic to humans. Recycled plastic lumber, especially when combined with wood fiber or other strengthening components, is another good alternative to CCA-treated lumber.

Recycled wood fiber (hardboard) siding and trim saves costs, is more stable than natural wood, and holds paint better. These hardboard products can lose durability in wet climates, though, if they are not installed properly.

Fiber-cement siding is extremely durable and looks like wood when painted. It is also fire resistant. The wood fibers lend elasticity and improve paint durability. Past problems with freeze-thaw damage in cold climates have been resolved.

Locally produced brick and stone can be excellent exterior choices. They are long-lasting, easy to maintain, and reduce transportation costs and environmental impacts. Molded cementitious stone, an alternative to natural stone, does not carry the environmental consequences of quarrying and transport associated with natural stone, but it adds to air pollution because it is made of cement.

Insulation

The environmental effects of insulation are greater than most other building materials. The level and quality of installation make a major difference in the amount of energy a house requires for heating and cooling. In general, more is better, and tighter is better, with a few caveats. For example, adding increased insulation to a ceiling is beneficial only if it is installed appropriately. A California study concluded that a 4 percent void in a fiberglass installation resulted in a 50 percent decrease  in insulation effectiveness. In another study, one wall section was framed with wood 2x4s insulated with fiberglass batts; another was framed with steel 2x4s, insulated with the same amount of fiberglass, and sheathed in 1" foam board. Results showed a 35 percent greater heat loss through the steel wall section because of the thermal conductivity of the steel (Oak Ridge Study).

Fiberglass is the standard insulation in the industry today. High-density fiberglass makes the same wall cavity 15-20 percent more effective than low density R=11 batts in reducing heat loss. Fiberglass can incorporate 10-30 percent recycled material in its manufacture. However, the problem of microparticulate shedding (the release of invisible fiberglass particles that can irritate people's skin, eyes, and lungs has become controversial). Loose fill is a greater risk than batts. In addition, fiberglass batts often use formaldehyde as a binder. Some newer products, though, employ alternative binders or no binders at all.

Cellulose insulation is environmentally friendly because it is primarily made from newsprint and recycled wood fiber from pre- and post-consumer waste. Another advantage is that when it is sprayed, it forms a good infiltration barrier, which adds to the tightness of the house and reduces drafts. It is less contractor-dependent for quality control in filling voids. Cellulose can be blown dry, mixed with a binder, or sprayed wet.

Rigid foam insulation applied to framing yields added infiltration resistance, reduced frame conduction losses, and added effective total wall R-value. Most rigid foams now are CFC free, using HCFCs as a blowing agent instead. Although much better than CFCs, HCFCs still contribute to ozone depletion and slowly outgas over time from the insulation. As a greenhouse gas, HCFCs are 150-500 times worse that CO_2 in contributing to global warming, though their work as insulator/energy-saver typically more than offsets their damage.[16]

Keep in mind that the more insulation installed in the house, the tighter the house becomes, the higher the possibility of creating indoor air quality problems. When your house is tested it should have greater than .35 air changes per hour (that is, the entire volume of air in the house is exchanged with outside air once every 3 hours). Anything less than that requires ventilation to provide fresh air to inhabitants.

Roofing

Petrochemical components are still used as the base for most residential roof composition shingle products. These products are not resource friendly, though, because they last for only 15 or 20 years and are rarely recycled. Forty-year shingles are a better choice. Alternatives are available in metal, plastic, and cement. These products use recycled content materials and come in shake or shingle-looking styles. Weight is an issue, though, with some of the cement-based roof tiles. Where hail is not a major threat, clay and concrete tiles are an option. All of the alternative roofing products have longer life spans than asphalt or fiberglass shingles and can be recycled.

A roof's durability is of key importance. Not only can roof failure cause serious damage to the roof itself, water is often destructive to the building and its contents. Failures tend to occur at joints and penetrations, so not only must the roofing material be durable, but the whole underlying system must be stable, including flashing and edge treatments.

Roofing can reduce home cooling costs and can affect the temperature of the surrounding yard and even the neighborhood. A Department of Energy program aimed at lowering ambient outdoor temperatures in urban and suburban areas recommends that builders use light-colored roofing surfaces, which absorb less heat than conventional roofing. Along with ceiling insulation, reflective roofing can significantly reduce summertime solar gain into the building and thereby reduce the need for artificial cooling.

Doors

Exterior doors are basically solid wood or foam wrapped in metal or some other weather-resistant material. Doors with foam insulation, except those made from expanded polystyrene, contain HCFCs. Most insulated doors are similar in energy efficiency since the market is so competitive. The key component is good weather stripping and an effective threshold. R-values of 5-7 are common.

Interior doors are usually wood, molded hardboard, or hollow core. Luan plywood is harvested from rain forests, so it should be avoided. Molded hardboard is often made with recycled material and pressed into shape, but some is made with urea-formaldehyde and should be avoided. Solid wood is a beautiful value-added product, but clear stock is becoming harder to get and often comes from old-growth forests.

Windows

Windows are one of the most high-tech products in residential construction. Over the last 15 years the effective R-value of windows has increased by 50 percent.

This is the result of improvements in glazing and frame construction. The National Fenestration Rating Council publishes a book, *The NFRC Certified Products Directory*, that rates overall window energy performance.

Although they have been a standard for many years, aluminum windows are phasing out of most cold climate areas and are being replaced by vinyl frames due to vinyl's higher R-value. Vinyl comes in a wide variety of qualities, however. Many frames have weather sealing problems over the life of the window due to expansion and contraction of the plastic. Some frame styles are prone to warping and sagging and are better suited to sliders and double hung styles than casements.

For energy efficiency, wood windows are still the standard, but manufacturers are facing the problem of finding affordable clear material with which to manufacture their product. Vinyl cladding adds value with its low maintenance qualities. Some manufacturers are using finger-jointed material with an interior coating and exterior cladding.

Low-E glass coating, which increases glass R-value from 2 to 3 is increasing in market share each year. The premium of 10-15 percent additional cost for low-E easily pays for itself in a few years. The added benefit is that in cold weather the window is warmer and therefore more comfortable to be near. Double low-E and HeatMirror are available in premium windows and can increase the R-value of the center-of-glass to 8.

Thought should go into placing low-E coated windows to maximize temperature regulation. In hot climates, choose coatings that transmit less solar gain. In cold climates, windows with glazing that allows more solar gain are desirable for south facing windows. East and west facing windows should minimize solar gain because sunlight is only intense in those directions during the summer. Thermal performance of windows can also be improved through using an inert gas such as argon or krypton between layers of glazing because these gases are less conductive than air.

Flooring and Floor Covering

Flooring should be durable to withstand daily use and to minimize the frequency with which it needs to be replaced. There is often a trade-off between hard floor coverings that are durable and easy to clean, and softer surfaces such as carpet, which provide more comfort and noise control, but tend to harbor more pollutants.

Vinyl tile and other sheet flooring products whose primary component is polyvinyl chloride (PVC) have the potential for VOC off-gassing. In addition, toxic by-products are produced in their manufacture. Natural linoleum, made primarily from flax and linseed oil, is an excellent substitute and one of the more environmentally friendly products available.

Ceramic and porcelain tiles are durable and therefore environmentally sound in the long run. Some high quality ceramic tile even contains recycled windshield glass in the glazing.

Carpet is a potential source of indoor air pollution, but a joint effort between the Carpet and Rug Institute and the EPA called the Green Label program identifies carpets that have reduced VOC emissions. A wide variety of high quality carpets are manufactured from recycled products such as recycled pop bottles (PET). Recycled content carpet has the performance and feel of conventional nylon carpet and is often more stain resistant.

Carpet tiles are another sustainable approach to carpeting because they can be replaced individually as needed. Carpet tiles also reduce waste and save money. These tiles often have a high recycled material content, and they can be resurfaced and reused. Some carpet recycling programs exist, and recycling usually costs no more than other disposal procedures.

The **underlayment** used between a sub-floor and floor covering is an environmental concern. Luan plywood, which is harvested unsustainably in Southeast Asia, is frequently used for underlayment, thus alternatives are preferred. Major tile manufacturers recommend a recycled-content, formaldehyde-free, gypsum-based underlayment.

When gluing down carpets, always use low-VOC adhesives or choose an alternative. For instance, you can use tack strips or a hook-and-loop tape system, which allows sections of carpet to be removed and replaced. A peel-and-stick acrylic adhesive is commonly used with carpet tiles.

Paints, Coatings, and Adhesives

These products, more than any others, can adversely affect indoor air quality, especially just after installation. The health hazard is particularly acute for installers. Most conventional products off-gas volatile organic compounds (VOCs), formaldehyde, and other chemicals that are generally used to enhance the performance and shelf life of the product. Medical research has raised concern, though, about the toxicity of combined chemicals on human health.[17]

Quality substitutions are now available for all these products. Some paints and adhesives use plant-based solvents. While these still off-gas VOCs, many people find them less troublesome than those emitted by petrochemicals.

Most VOCs from wet-applied products are released while the product dries, but they can continue to emit VOCs for long periods of time. Additionally, soft surfaces such as fabrics and carpets can absorb these VOCs and reemit them. To minimize extended release of VOCs, remove or cover all soft surfaces and employ direct ventilation until the coating dries.

For wood floor finishes, water-based urethane is suggested. This product contains no cross-linkers (a variety of toxic chemicals that add hardness). Other water-based finishes are also available. They can be as durable as standard solvent-based finishes, and installers often prefer them because they are less harmful to workers.

Interior Finish and Trim

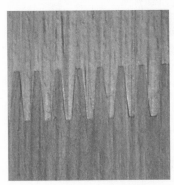

Particleboard is a potential health problem due to bonding agents that use urea-formaldehyde, which can off-gas VOCs for years after application. However, an alternative medium density fiberboard (MDF) that contains no formaldehyde exists for cabinet construction and trim. Cabinets made with non-toxic materials and finishes, solid wood, and enameled metal are also available.

Clear material for wood trim is increasingly scarce and expensive. Finger-jointed material is generally available in most trim profiles when it is to be painted. For stain grade material, veneer coated, finger-jointed trim is available in several grades and wood species types.

Solid wood products, interior finish, and trim should originate from certified well-managed forests when possible. The Forest Stewardship Council and the Rainforest Alliance (Smartwood: See Appendix B for more information) are two U.S. organizations that certify forest operations. Again, because tropical forests are such delicate ecosystems, tropical hardwoods should be avoided unless they come from certified sustainable forests.

Conclusions

What conclusions can we draw from this information?

➔ Make green solutions clear to your customers. Many Americans are increasingly concerned about their lack of control over the pollutants they breathe. The products you choose for the interiors of their homes can give them confidence in the health of their home environment. These products can help prevent various respiratory problems in adults and children.

➔ Not all movements toward sustainability require lifestyle changes. Installing water-efficient appliances in your homes will give your buyers the conveniences they are accustomed to, save them money in the long run, and also conserve one of our most precious resources.

➔ As a builder, you are in a powerful position to influence the trends of environmental degradation. You can choose to use only sustainably-harvested lumber. Home Depot has made the commitment to sell only such lumber. Or, for example, every day in the U.S. more energy flows out of our windows and is lost than is brought in on the Alaska pipeline.[18] By simply specifying Low-E windows with a higher R-value, you are essentially creating energy. In turn, you reduce the quantity of greenhouse gasses entering the atmosphere because the home will require less energy for heating. Realizing that constructing the average home results in three to five tons of waste, you can be overwhelmed, or you can see this as an opportunity to recycle job-site waste. Your efforts to reduce, reuse, and recycle could have notable effects on the space available at your local landfill, lessen the strain on natural resources, and reduce your costs.

➤ In order to transition into a practice of building green, one of the primary changes we as builders need to make is to change our perspective from the short term to the long term. We need to consider the ramifications of our choices into the future.

➤ The choice of green material selection requires many considerations that have to be driven by good business sense. How many substitutions can you incorporate and still stay competitive? How will green improve your sales and marketing? Can each decision you make be a win-win for your buyers and your business?

In essence, every decision you make about what materials you use either leads toward a more sustainable future or decreases the opportunities for future generations to live lifestyles that we have come to take for granted.

Moving toward sustainable development is a process that involves new ways of thinking and building. Yet the question is not really how to become more sustainable—the knowledge and technology exist to guide us in the appropriate actions to take. The question is when?

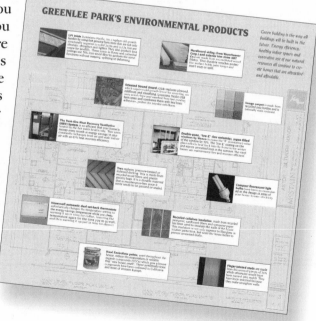

Now that you are more aware of what green building is, take a look at Section 2 - Becoming a Green Builder, which shows you how to become a green builder step-by-step.

Endnotes

1. Colin J. Campbell and Jean H. Laherrère, "The End of Cheap Oil," *Scientific American* (March 1998).

2. J. Potting and K. Blok, "The Environmental Life-cycle Analysis of Floor Coverings," (1993).

3. John Bower, The Healthy House Institute.

4. Wayne Ott and John Roberts, "Everyday Exposure to Toxic Pollutants," *Scientific American* (February, 1998).

5. Ibid.

6. Arthur C. Upton, MD (National Institutes of Health), *Staying Healthy in a Risky Environment* (New York: Simon and Shuster, 1993).

7. David Malin Roodman and Nicholas Lenssen, "A Building Revolution: How Ecology and Health Concerns are Transforming Construction" (Worldwatch Paper 124, March 1995).

8. World Resources Institute "Temperate and Boreal Forests" 10/21/99 <http://www.wri.org/biodiv/temperat.html>

9. William P. Cunningham and Barbara Woodworth Saigo, *Environmental Science: A Global Concern* (Dubuque, IA: William C. Brown Publishers, 1997).

10. Ibid, p.295.

11. Donald Prowler, *The Case for the Modest Mansion* (Emmaus PA: Rodale Press, 1986).

12. Cunningham Saigo, *Environmental Science: A Global Concern*, p.466.

13. Ibid, p.423.

14. Steve Loken, Rod Minor, and Tracy Mumma, *A Reference Guide to Resource Efficient Building Elements, 4th ed.* (Missoula, MT: Center for Resourceful Building Technology, 1994), p.7.

15. Ibid, p.8.

16. National Oceanic and Atmospheric Administration, "Issue of the Global Environmental Change Report" (June 14, 1996).

17. The following books are excellent sources of more information on indoor air quality: *The Healthy Household*, by Lynn Marie Bower, 1995; *Prescriptions for a Healthy House: A Practical Guide for Architects, Builders, and Homeowners*, by Paula Baker, AIA, Erica Elliott, MD, and John Banta, 1998; and *Chemical Exposures: Low Levels and High Stakes*, by Nicholas A. Ashford and Claudia S. Miller, 1991.

18. Janet Marinelli and Paul Bierman-Lytle, *Your Natural Home: A Complete Sourcebook and Design Manual for Creating a Healthy, Beautiful, Environmentally Sensitive House* (New York: Little, Brown and Company, 1995), p.141-142.

3

How to
Enter the Market

Green building is an incremental process that begins with how you are currently building. This chapter evaluates the approaches you can take, the products you can start with, the cost implications, and addresses the market.

Start Where You Are - By determining your local market conditions you can decide on which green features will be the most desirable in your area. Begin by giving your customers choices of different green option packages.

Actual Costs—Is Green Building Too Expensive? - This section includes an itemized breakdown of costs for homes with different environmental packages. This information helps alleviate fears about the cost of incorporating green features into homes.

Taking Your First Steps - Making your transition to being a green builder at a moderate pace ensures that all your products and practices have integrity.

Sales and Marketing - Two important keys to sales and marketing are being aware of market trends and telling the story behind the green features you are using.

Hopefully, after reading the first section, you have a solid understanding of what green building is and you are intrigued about the market possibilities for going green. Section 2 - How to Become a Green Builder, takes you through the steps to make those market possibilities your reality. There is no right way to begin other than with experimentation. Each market is different and will respond best to a different set of green product selections. At the same time, many builders from across the country have blazed the trail for green building and have learned lessons that can save you time and headaches. The key is to start carefully so that building green brings "the green" to your bottom line.

John Knott, Dewees Island
Isle of Palms, S. Carolina
(800) 886-8783
www.deweesisland.com

John Knott, a third-generation builder, is the managing director and CEO of the Island Preservation Partnership, developer of Dewees Island, South Carolina. Dewees is an oceanfront island retreat dedicated to environmental preservation and a model of profitable sustainable development (See case study in Chapter 9). Knott has extensive experience in the development of planned communities, commercial offices, hotels, and in the renovation/restoration of historic properties and city redevelopment. He served as Chairman of the White House Exchange with the Soviet Union for City Redevelopment/Historic Preservation. In addition, Knott was the founder and Chairman of the Executive board for the Harmony Project, a non-profit foundation promoting the development of sustainable communities.

John Knott addresses the question, why build green?: "What are the incentives that will encourage a builder to start building green? Number one, you end up making more money. Because you are using resources more efficiently, the building is more durable, and the people are healthier in it. This translates into higher profits for your company. You are going to have fewer call-backs, which means your warranty costs are going to be far less."

Knott also says that if you can get your trades and suppliers excited about being part of a green building program, they will commit themselves to deliver a higher quality product. In addition, and maybe most importantly, he says, "you feel good about yourself and what you are building."

One easy step: Hire a green building consultant who has had experience getting other builders started. Often a consultant will have more diverse experience than a single builder. Good green building consultants across the country can bring you a wealth of market experience, product familiarity, and insight into what sells and what doesn't.

Start Where You Are

It is best to start where your market is now and work from there. If you start gradually, you won't make expensive mistakes, and you will learn what does and doesn't work for you.

Local Market Conditions

Your experience is your best guide. You know what your customers want because you have successfully built and sold homes for years. Building differently takes careful consideration of the changes you will make and the additional costs you might incur in the process. Starting to build green requires your best judgment at every step. What customers want in Colorado or California is different from what they want in Michigan or Iowa. In the West, water conservation and clean air are major opportunities to address. In the Mid-West, where energy is expensive and the climate is cold, builders have been improving energy efficiency for years. Energy may not be the best way to differentiate yourself in such locations. But through increasing energy efficiency, your competition may have inadvertently created indoor air quality problems by building tighter homes. Therefore, building homes that emphasize good indoor air quality might be just the thing to get your buyers' attention.

At the same time, homebuyers don't always know what they want. They know what they like when they see it, but if no green options are available, and if no model homes include green features, they may not realize that they have a choice.

—— Give Your Customers Choices ——

Giving your customers a choice in materials and design is a safe way to start. Define a green option package for your buyers that clearly describes the environmental features and benefits, and see how they respond.

Energy Conservation Package

➜ Many builders have created an energy conservation package as an upgrade. Energy conserving features typically save the homeowner money every month in utility bills. These features can also increase the affordability of the home by qualifying them for an energy-efficient mortgage.

An Energy Conservation Package might include:
- **Insulated foundation**
- **2x6 wall framing with increased insulation**
- **Advanced sealing and caulking to reduce drafts**
- **Low-E windows**
- **High efficiency furnace and hot water heater**

Indoor Air Quality Package

➜ Good indoor air quality is translated into a healthy living environment for the family. Remember that a significant portion of the market is health conscious, as the sales of organic produce and bottled water show. You can promote healthy indoor air quality as an attractive feature. And it is often a low- or no-cost option.

An Indoor Air Quality package might include:
- **Low-toxic adhesives**
- **No VOC paints**
- **Water based wood floor finishes**
- **Linoleum upgrade from vinyl tile**
- **Limited use of particleboard in cabinets and countertops**

Resource Conservation Package

➲ Knowing that they are conserving natural resources is less likely to appeal
to some consumers than improved indoor
air quality, but it can be an attractive sales
message to environmentally conscious consumers. Conserving resources can also
appeal to your buyers' children, who often
have more influence than you may think in
their parents' final purchase decision.

**A Resource Conservation Package
might include:**

- **Engineered lumber–OSB, wood I-joists, laminated
  veneer lumber**
- **Recycled newsprint cellulose insulation**
- **Hardboard siding and trim**
- **Recycled content decking**
- **Pop-bottle carpet**
- **Water conserving plumbing fixtures**

Pulling the Green Package Together

You can experiment by offering just one of these packages, or
you can offer all three as separate options packages to test your
buyers' and prospective buyers' interests. Your green package
could, of course, include a combination of all three options.

➲ Complement each package with a list of benefits of each
feature, not just the list of components. Buyers can relate to
the benefits but often don't know a wood I-joist from a garage
door opener (see Chapter 6).

Tom Hoyt, president of McStain Enterprises, says, "We realized
that you can't just give people the option of an energy saving
light fixture and have them understand it in the context of the
whole building package. When we started working with an environmental construction consultant, it was about how to put it all
together—what were the components that created the most
value for the customer?"

Telling Your Green Story

The key point is to tell the story of your green package. Buyers
are fascinated with a commentary like: "My son came home from
school one day and asked me why I was cutting down all the old
trees. I told him I didn't cut down any trees. He replied, 'But Dad,

you build houses, and in school they said that houses use most of the old trees, and when I grow up there won't be any left.' The first thing I did was straighten him out about reforestation. I told him there were more trees today than when the pilgrims landed. Then, I started thinking about what he said. Perhaps there was a

COURTESY OF CYNDRA DIETZ/ECO-CYCLE

way to build without using any old growth trees. I had been using some engineered lumber products but still used 2x10s for floor joists. Our company decided to build forest-friendly homes and plant trees on Arbor Day. Mr. & Mrs. Jones, you can feel good about living in this house, because more trees were planted than were cut to build it." A story like this personalizes what it means to you to build green and makes you stand out from other builders who couldn't care less about such things.

—— Pricing Options ——

Pricing options is a tricky proposition. When green is carefully designed into the home from the start, potential incremental costs can often be reduced. Energy savings can offset the increased cost of the monthly mortgage payment (see cost section below) so that the homeowner's net monthly payment is nearly the same. When additional costs for green options do exist, they can be incorporated into the base price, and the monthly mortgage payment increase will be negligible.

When green features are offered as an option package, identify the additional costs. You might want to start by reducing mark-up on the initial green offering to gauge the reaction of your buyers. Some customers, of course, would rather put additional money into a whirlpool tub in the master bedroom or a cabinet upgrade in the kitchen. Let them know their options. Tell them that such improvements are comparable in cost to a total green upgrade. As always, it is how you present the packages that sells them. When the customer believes the benefits outweigh an additional few dollars a month, it is often an easy sell.

Peter Pfeiffer, an Austin, Texas, architect, was one of the early proponents of green building in Austin. With 28 years of experience under his belt, he finds: "It doesn't have to cost more to build green, and it will provide a marketing edge. It may actually save clients money. Fewer recessed light fixtures, smaller air conditioning units, low pitched roofs, and properly placed windows can reduce the cost of the job. Stained and scored concrete floors save flooring costs, reduce dust, and improve indoor air quality. I always sell comfort over features."

Peter Pfeiffer
Barley & Pfeiffer Architects
Austin, Texas
(512) 476-8580
Peter Pfeiffer spent 15 years in the design and construction industry before opening his sustainable architecture firm in 1987. Pfeiffer specializes in sustainable design and energy consulting and has focused much of his career on developing practical methods to "mainstream" green building. In addition, Pfeiffer serves as an advisor to the City of Austin's internationally recognized "Green Builder Program." In 1994, the Energy Efficient Building Association awarded Pfeiffer their Conference Chair's Award for his career accomplishments in pioneering environmentally sensitive architecture.

Costs, Contractors, and Products

⚠ A caution with option packages: When trades contractors have to go back and forth between conventional products and green substitutions, that can cause confusion. If they are used to using one product and you require them to use another, you may encounter some resistance.

⚠ Making the change might also require additional supervision, which is another cost increase. If some of these changes become standard practice, however, you can often get quantity price discounts from suppliers. This helps reduce the incremental costs of new products and encourages your suppliers to carry them on a continual basis.

Bill Eich, of Spirit Lake, Iowa, has been building green homes for years. He relates this story: "The costs of building green came to a head on an entry-level home. We were competing with a modular home and there was a difference between our bids of $1500-$2000 because of our airtight construction approach. The crew got together and said, 'Don't give them the option. Give them the upgrade, and we will do the work to bring the cost down through increased performance. We won't build a house wrong anymore.'

From then on it has never been an option, it's just the way we build."

The moral of the story is that isolating green costs can be an illusion. There are many variables that determine the final cost to the consumer. Labor productivity can easily off-set increases in material costs. Also, with good design, savings in one area can balance out increases in another.

One Builder's Advice

Jim Van Derhyden, describes Investec's process: "My goal is to build green for the mass market, not solely for the upper crust who want to be politically correct. It doesn't do any good if 2 percent of the houses in the country are green and the other 98 percent aren't. But if you get to a point where 30-40 percent of the houses in the country are incorporating sustainable methods into their construction, then you are going to start making some difference in the world."

Jim Van Derhyden
Investec Construction
Santa Barbara, California
(805) 962-7828

Jim Van Derhyden is Vice President of Investec Construction, a multifaceted real estate company involved in all aspects of real estate. In the early 1990s, Investec got involved in homebuilding along the central California coast, primarily in Santa Barbara and San Luis Obispo. They started using green building practices due to governmental incentives to reduce processing time for exceeding energy efficiency requirements. Investec's commitment to green principles has facilitated approvals for them to build in areas highly opposed to growth, while at the same time meeting the sophisticated demands of their buyers.

Van Derhyden says that everything is bottom line. When he tells people about the advantages of green building, they'll often say, "Oh, but it costs more." He tells them that it doesn't have to. He says that planning makes all the difference. Building green is a thought process that starts in the beginning so that the systems are designed with whole house in mind. And in the end, what some people would say is dumb luck, is really good design. The number one goal for his company is that the bottom line cost stays the same. The consumer gets a much better product, the house will save energy over its 30-50 year life, and it will have fewer mechanical problems.

Costs vary with every builder and by geographic location. But some approaches can be generalized. The following section discusses one way to understand how to approach the additional costs of green building.

Actual Costs - Is Building Green Too Expensive?

Builders often claim that building green is too expensive and that they can't afford to incorporate the green features. They also claim that when they increase the cost of the home, they lose the lower income families who can't qualify for the higher priced home. Although it is possible to add costs that exclude buyers, the following analysis shows how to add the features that customers want and increase the percentage of buyers who can qualify for the home.

The following study was conducted for the redevelopment of the old Stapleton airport site in Denver. It began with focus groups and an analysis of what prospective homebuyers wanted. The cost breakdowns were directed at several areas of consumer interest: What's in it for me? How can I save money? How can I protect my children with a healthier home? and other environmental or "feel good" options.

This study is based on a 1540 square foot home typical of the market average in the Denver neighborhood adjacent to Stapleton. The house is two stories with an unfinished basement. It is front loaded with an attached two-car garage. It has 3 bedrooms and 2 baths. The sales price of the original model is $150,000.

The following costs reflect materials only. They were based on the builders' costs for conventional materials, and where green features were more expensive, only the additional cost is identified.

Stapleton Environmental Option Packages

OPTION PACKAGE 1 (What's in it for me?)	Cost

Energy Features:

1. Enhanced sealing package	$230
Spray foam seals cracks to reduce drafts	
2. Spray-cellulose insulation	$150
Recycled newsprint further reduces infiltration	
3. Suntempering	$0
Existing windows moved to south wall	
Southern windows help heat the home	
4. Energy efficient hot water heater (DHW)	$275
R=16 tank jacket reduces heat loss	
5. Set-back thermostat	$75
Night temperature reduction saves energy	
6. Low-E Windows	$185
Coating saves heat and improves comfort	
7. Ceiling fan	$300

Green Features, reduced maintenance:

1. Recycled content decking	$163
30 yr. life/no painting required	
2. Recycled content carpet	$0
Longer lasting, more stain resistant	
3. Xeriscaping	$0
Water saving, less maintenance	

Other no or minimal cost green features

1. Recycled content siding	$0
Less repainting, more durable	
2. Engineered lumber	$200
Eliminates old growth framing lumber,	
Creates a stronger, straighter home	

Total additional cost Option 1	**$1578**

Energy upgrade features result in an estimated annual utility savings of $185. The amortized carrying costs of the upgrades at an 8% mortgage rate is $139, resulting in an annual savings of $46 for the family.

OPTION PACKAGE 2 (Will my home be healthy?)   Cost

Health Features

1. Low-toxic adhesives	$23
Eliminating toxins in conventional glues	
2. Sealing particleboard cabinets and counter top	$250
Seals in formaldehyde, prevents out-gassing	
3. VOC free paint	$100
No harmful VOCs inside home	
4. Water-based finishes on wood and floors	$150
Lowered toxic solvents in floor finish	

Total additional cost Option 2 $523

Based on a $150,000 priced home, additional costs for Option 1 + Option 2 of $2101= 1.4 percent added to price ($152,101).

The total annual carrying costs for Options 1+2 = $185. This is equivalent to the energy savings from Option 1.

OPTION PACKAGE 3 (additional beneficial features) Cost

Energy Features:

1. High efficiency furnace & DHW	$1000
Saves energy with 90%+ efficiency	
2. Passive solar features	$1350
30% energy savings with south windows	
Add recycled tile for thermal mass	
3. Above code insulation	$1000
R=24 walls (1" foam wrap), R=38 ceilings	
4. High efficiency appliances	$500
$100-200/yr. savings	
5. Compact fluorescent lighting	$200
Electricity savings, bulbs last 4 times longer	
Total energy upgrade	**$4,050**

Additional Green Features:

1. Cement based roofing	$3850
Fire insurance savings, 50 year life	
2. Cement based siding	$250
No maintenance, fire resistant, 50 year life	
3. Recycled content ceramic tile	$375
More durable floors	
Total green upgrade	**$4,475**

Additional Health Features:

1. Formaldehyde-free sub floors	$600
No off- gassing from adhesives	
2. Formaldehyde-free cabinets and counters	$600
No off- gassing from cabinets into food	
3. Heat recovery ventilation	$1000
Year 'round fresh air, vents indoor toxins	
Eliminates furnace, heats home with DHW	
Total health upgrade	**$2,200**
Total additional cost Option 3	**$10,725**

The additional energy features result in an estimated energy savings (including Option 1) of $70-100 per year, depending on the extent of passive solar contribution. The additional carrying cost for all Option 3 features is $856 per year.

Based on the $150,000 house, additional costs = 6.5 percent added to the price. With all options, the total is $162,826 (some features are redundant and reductions would be made to total cost depending on features chosen).

A typical family with a combined annual income of $48,000 could qualify for a $150,000 home. By incorporating just some of the energy features, the buyer could qualify for an Energy Efficient Mortgage. (This mortgage program factors in principal, interest, taxes, and insurance, plus energy bills, PITI+E.) The program allows a "stretch" of 2 percent increase in the buyer's debt-to-income ratio, so the same family could qualify for a $163,000 home and use all three option packages above for $162,826.

➲ This example of costs associated with green building illustrates that not only can you incorporate the features your customers want, but you can do it so that even more buyers can qualify for your home by taking advantage of the Energy Efficient Mortgage program. Energy conservation helps sell homes by making them more affordable monthly and by helping lower income families get better housing.

Taking Your First Steps

The first steps in becoming a green builder are surprisingly easy. Your company may already be incorporating many green products.

➲ 1. Use one of the checklists from HBA green programs and conduct a self-evaluation of the materials you currently use. The Denver checklist is a comprehensive list that can give you a good idea of how you are doing. (See Appendix A.)

- Are you using engineered lumber, wood I-joists, microlams, or OSB?
- Are you building energy conserving homes now?
- Do you install high efficiency HVAC equipment?

In many markets these products and approaches are commonplace.

➲ 2. Don't go whole hog the first time out. Green building is an evolutionary process that takes time to develop. Get comfortable with each new set of products. Do some research. You might want to create a research house, as in the example below.

McStain's Tom Hoyt says, "With our research house we asked: What packages can we assemble that will give customers real value and give them the sense that they are contributing towards environmental improvement?"

To answer this question, McStain researched all the potentials and developed a prototype house. As a production builder, their greatest fear was that they would put something in a house fifty times, then find out it failed and that they were responsible. They already had costly examples of that, and it was difficult on customer relationships.

The research house gave the company the opportunity to evaluate all the potentials and decide on the best collection of items.

After looking into various options, they narrowed their focus down to energy efficiency, indoor air quality, and building material sustainability. With several consultants' help, they developed a set of options that they put into one of their production houses. This exercise was a valuable experience. They found materials that their trades contractors refused to install. They discovered products that were supposed to be available but weren't. Some materials supposedly cost one thing but cost something else. Some approaches worked extremely well that they didn't know would. (See Chapter 7 for the case study.)

If your market research shows that indoor air quality and children's health are of interest to your customers, for example, pay attention to that. Do the easy things first. Take your time.

➡ 3. Start with low-cost features and identify those that will require little change in your current process. Low-VOC paints and finishes are a good first step. Once you have tried some of the new products, it is easy to make them standard practice.

➡ 4. After you have worked your way up to qualifying for one of the green building programs, you can establish yourself as a green builder through your company presentation and brochures. Be confident in your package and credible in the combination of features you have chosen. The consumer is often more aware of green issues than you might think and is sensitive to "greenwashing," which is the claim of being more environmental than is really true. (See Chapter 6 for brochure and sales information.)

➡ 5. A footnote: experiment with the products you think might become part of your green package. Test them in your garage, on your mother-in-law, or on "freebee" jobs for your neighbors. Develop a comfort level first then offer them to your customers.

Tom Hoyt says, "One piece of advice I'd give is to educate your people, especially if you are going to use something innovative." Let them know what you are doing, Hoyt suggests. Involve them in researching and engineering the products so they perform the way you think they are going to.

Sales and Marketing

Selling what you build is the most important aspect of building green.

➡ Tell the story behind each product that you use. Emphasize that green doesn't necessarily cost more. Tell your customers that green options can qualify them for a larger house. Realtors and sales personnel don't often show a customer the kind of cost breakdown and analysis used in the above study. Yet, when these are explained to the customer, green options can be a powerful sales tool.

——— Benefits Sell Homes ———

Buyers love stories, and green features provide opportunities to tell stories about the house and the features that make it green. Even if it is just a list of benefits (see Chapter 6 for benefits list), you will be doing something different from your competition, and you will leave a lasting impression on your buyers. Green features

may not sell the home at first blush, but they will make buyers think and will often bring them back. And remember that many buyers are more sophisticated than you may realize. *Better Homes and Gardens*, *Redbook*, *Family Circle*, and other magazines that highlight home improvement have covered issues of indoor air quality and green building for years. As a result, your buyers may know more about your homes and the products you use than you do.

For example, several years ago I taught a green building workshop for realtors. During the question and answer period a realtor stood up and told this story:

"I was sitting in an open house for my builder a couple of weeks ago. A woman came in and asked if I would show her the house. Of course I started toward the kitchen, when she said, 'I would like to start in the basement.' I was shocked but accommodated her wishes. When we got down there she looked up at the 2x10

floor joists and asked how many old growth trees were used in the house. I had no idea what she was talking about and mumbled something to the effect of only using good wood for all the framing. When we finally got back upstairs (territory I was comfortable with) she started sniffing around the place. I asked her what she was doing. She wanted to know what caused the 'new house smell' and how much formaldehyde there was in the house. I was clueless. There was a pregnant pause after which she said, 'I don't think this is the house for us.' I told the story to the builder, and he insisted on my coming to this seminar. I think both of us will do things differently next time."

It doesn't take many encounters of that kind to make your sales people think about the green aspects of new homes. That realtor lost a prospective sale by not knowing the issues and therefore not being ready for an informed buyer. A brief introduction to green building issues is in everyone's best interest. If the sales staff are prepared and know how to sell the features, they can close a sale that might otherwise have gotten away. (See Chapter 6 for other sales suggestions.)

Tom Hoyt's advice for getting started:

➤ Focus your priorities into something doable. Don't set your objectives too high.

➤ Look at your position relative to the rest of the marketplace and evaluate what you think might differentiate you. Take the basic pieces of green building—energy conservation, indoor air quality, and sustainable resource use—and assess your strengths. Maybe you know your competitors have indoor air quality problems due to the products they use. You could stand out from them by focusing on indoor air quality.

➲ Assess your market for what people care about. Use your own customers—you have a tremendous resource in the people you've sold houses to, whether you're a custom builder or a production builder who sells two or three hundred homes per year. Go back to your buyers and ask them what they care about. Discover what will make the most difference.

➲ I highly advise people to read their newspaper, and not just the real estate section. It's important to be aware of general market trends. Understand that air quality is a concern for a lot of people. Narrow down the trends you see to what you think your organization can handle.

➲ Include your people in the process. Make it very clear that green building is a priority for you. Show them that you have the vision. Involve them in practical steps to accomplish your vision.

➲ The minute you've made a commitment to green building, you've got to focus on what you are doing. If you make a hundred changes, you've got a thousand decisions to make. The minute you open the door, there are lots of choices, so don't open the door too widely at first. Try a few changes at a time.

Conclusion

Lee Kitson, gives this advice on how to get started: "Go to a workshop, get a book on green building, and listen to other builders who have done it. Learn how they succeeded. There are many things that you may have not thought about, like how to tie the whole package together into a green sales approach. My sense is that there is interest in these things. You have to spend some additional money on marketing, but there are people in every market who agree that green building is important."

Lee Kitson, Kitson Builders
Rockford (Grand Rapids), Michigan
(616) 863-9090
Kitson Builders is a family business with twelve employees. Kitson builds 35 to 40 homes per year (25-30 in exclusive subdivisions and 10-12 on scattered lots). They are involved in recycling and incorporate green features into their homes. Currently, Kitson is developing a 15-lot site and is building green homes on all the lots.

Starting the process of building green can be exciting, especially when your customers respond enthusiastically. However, green building is a balancing act. It requires looking at tradeoffs to determine what makes the most sense for your company.

In Jim Van Derhyden's words, "The bottom line is long-term survival, and green building is the right thing to do. If you're not in business, you can't do the right thing. So which comes first, the chicken or the egg? Stay in business and do the right thing, and make money doing it."

As always:

- Do good business.
- Keep a sharp eye on the bottom line.
- Make sure that your decisions are in your customer's best interests.

Now that you have taken a look at ways to enter the market, you may be ready to create a green company. The following chapter draws on the experience of other builders and offers guidelines for success.

Creating a Green Company

4

Using green products is only the first step. Integrating green into your whole organization is the best way to sustain your effort and capture the market. From design to punch-out, all the employees and trades contractors need to "buy-in" to the idea for the effort to be successful.

Creating a Vision - Determine the impact you want your company to make. Share your vision and ask for feedback.

Design - Green design is more than adding energy efficient features. Through an integrated design approach it incorporates the home into the larger ecosystem.

Aligning Employees' Jobs with Green Building - From superintendents to trades contractors to the sales team, communicate to your employees how green building benefits them.

Unless an organization sees that its task is to lead change, that organization (whether a business, a university, or a hospital) will not survive. In a period of rapid structural change the only organizations that survive are the "change leaders." It is therefore a central 21st century challenge for management that its organization become a change leader.

—Peter Drucker, "Change Leaders," *Inc.* Magazine, June 1999, from <u>Management Challenges for the 21st Century</u>, Harper Collins, 1999.

Becoming a green company is an opportunity to add value to your company by incorporating some of the strategies used by Fortune 100 companies to align their vision with their businesses and increase their bottom line. Corporate America has been undergoing a quiet revolution for a decade, and since then, the United States has become the most productive nation in the world.

Building A Better World

At McStain, we have a continuing commitment to:

- Design and build visionary communities that integrate the aesthetic, physical and emotional needs of our customers.

- Develop and build in a sustainable partnership with the natural environment.

- Treat our clients, employees, associates and the broader community we serve with respect and integrity.

McSTAIN

Management consultants like Peter Drucker have led the charge by guiding CEOs through the process of change. He now instructs them in how to become change leaders. Green builders are the change leaders in the building industry. By keeping one eye to the future and the other on the bottom line, you can learn how to do better business while creating a new market niche for your company.

Building a green company involves more than just using green products. For a green company to be successful and capture the market, all the employees and trades people need to buy-in to the green program and actively participate in it. One essential factor in achieving buy-in is to create a vision for your company. From the vision you create a mission statement, which establishes a framework for making decisions. Your mission statement is the glue that will hold the company together through time and employee turnover.

Creating the Vision

Tom and Caroline Hoyt have created an environmentally aware company culture that has sustained them over time. McStain Enterprises has been developing unique properties and building homes in Boulder, Colorado, for 35 years. The company has become an environmental construction icon in the eyes of the public and the building industry. The Hoyts attribute much of their success to their employees' contributions to the organization's vision. The company's mission statement is: "Building a better world."

Kristin Shewfelt, Director of Market Research and Environmental Programs for McStain, offers insight into developing a vision for your company. She says, "Sit down and figure out what you really want to do. What are your goals and objectives? Develop a sustainable vision for your company. Your vision provides guiding principles that you can use for years to come." Down the line when decisions need to be made, you can look to those principles to provide answers.

Tom Hoyt says, "The trick is to get your whole company to buy-in to that vision. Today especially, the advantage of having that kind of outlook is that most of your employees really want more than a good job and good pay and good benefits. They want to know they've got a purpose in this world."

When you make a commitment to green building, your employees feel like their job and their company are contributing to a greater purpose. It's powerful for them, it's powerful for you, and it's powerful for your customers. But it has been the convention in business, and especially the building business, not to think about those things, Hoyt says.

Studies show that employees today want effective leaders with a clear vision. Ron Kertzner of ChoicePoint Consultants, which provides management consulting to Fortune 100

Sue Jordan-Kertzner, Ron Kertzner ChoicePoint Consulting Inc. Boulder, Colorado
Sue Jordan-Kertzner and Ron Kertzner are CEO and president, respectively, of ChoicePoint Consulting. ChoicePoint is a consulting, coaching, and management education firm, which helps individuals and organizations create the results they truly desire. They focus on the following competencies: creating shared vision, personal mastery, collaboration, and conflict resolution, mental models, and emotional literacy.

companies, explains: "Since the 1950s the command-and-control style of leadership has been the dominant model, but now we are moving toward a more collaborative style of leadership.

Employees want their CEO to say, 'This is who we are, and this is where we are going.' And they want to be involved in creating the vision.' "

Sue Kertzner says, "To create a corporate vision, I would offer guidance for you, the CEO. We would sit down and figure out what your core values are, what impact you want your life to have, and what kind of legacy you want to leave with your company. Out of that thinking you would create a personal mission statement."

Once you have developed a personal mission statement, Sue says, make a list of values that would depict green for your company. Examples might include:

- What does it mean to be green?
- What other values are important—respect for the individual, respect for the client, respect for the environment?
- How would being green change your decision-making process?
- When potential customers call on the phone, what kinds of questions are you going to ask them?
- Why would being green be important to both you and your customers?

Then, Sue suggests, have a round of internal "town meetings." Start talking about your vision with the rest of the company.

Buy-in

I asked Ron Kertzner how to go about enrolling the whole organization in your vision and core values. He said, "The way you don't do it is through the edict approach: 'This is the way we are going to be!' That's a fallback to command-and-control management style. Sue and I saw a president of a large company stand in front of 700 employees at an annual meeting and declare, 'We will be a collaborative organization!' You can't start like that. Start with your vision. Then ask your people for their input, for their comments. Ask them what ideas they have about how to improve the way the company is operating."

Kertzner says to tell your people what your vision and values are for becoming a green company. Ask them:

- What about this do you like?
- What doesn't work for you?
- What do you need?
- What are your interests?

In the course of that conversation, you'll find out what their deeper concerns are. Maybe it's that when they build faster, using familiar conventional methods, they get bigger bonuses. So you think of new ways you could work your bonus system (create new criteria). And that's key: line up the compensation and reward systems with your values. Otherwise people won't buy in to the values.

• **Mini-workshops are valuable.** For example, employees can participate in personal vision and values exercises. They identify what is most important to them and see how strongly their values do or do not link up with the corporate vision.

• **Address is the company norms.** Have sessions with your employees and ask them: What are the unwritten rules of the game in this company? Then ask which norms would have to shift to align with the new vision. What you want to create is consistent behavior.

Managing the Difference Between Your Vision and Current Reality

Getting buy-in requires managing the creative tension that exists between your vision and the company's current reality. Speak clearly about the vision you want to create, but at the same time, tell the truth about where you are right now.

For instance, how do employees feel about the challenges you face in becoming green? Where is the green market now, versus where you would like it to be? Holding that tension between the current reality and your desired vision creates room in the middle for ideas, possibilities, and solutions, all of which will emerge and move you toward your vision.

Flexibility and Commitment

Achieving buy-in from employees demands that you be flexible in how you implement your vision, but at some point you have to draw the line and say, "This is what our company is about." After that, people will choose to buy-in or leave. The very nature of change will push some people out. Those who remain after the line is drawn, however, typically show higher productivity and strong commitment to the green vision.

──────── Implementation ────────

Too many companies stop at the vision stage. It is a mistake to believe that just creating a vision is sufficient to enroll all the staff in a new direction. Implementation requires follow-through,

CHANGE PROCESS MODEL

1. *Clarify your personal vision & core values*

2. *Write draft vision & value statements.*

3. *Hold "Town Meetings." Speak your vision & dialogue with employees.*

4. *Conduct employee workshops on values.*

5. *Hold "Building Commitment" sessions with employees.*

6. *Communicate vision & values in varied methods.*

7. *Align rewards system with vision & values.*

8. *Charter core process teams.*

9. *Identify measures of success.*

- *Monitor*
- *Communicate*
- *Refine*

FEEDBACK LOOP

On your way to lasting culture change!

patience, and good listening skills to really hear what your employees are feeling about the change. Change isn't easy for anyone, especially when wages are on the line.

Sue Kertzner says that since fear is inherent in implementing changes, you can do an exercise that addresses these fears. You or a consultant can run a corporate "town meeting." Have your employees brainstorm questions like:

- What if we took this new path of green building?
- What is the best case scenario of what our customers will experience?
- What would the community at large experience?
- How we would feel coming to work?

Then do the same process with these questions:

- What is the worst thing that could happen?
- What is the most probable?

Discussing different scenarios alleviates some of the fear because most fears are a fantasy about the future. The key to employee buy-in is to harness the excitement of creating a different kind of future with a different kind of company.

Credibility of the Leader is Important

Credibility is essential in implementing change. First, leaders need to take symbolic actions such as changing the smoking policy in the office to show they are really living their green values. Credibility is also developed when leaders are open to the fact that, like all of us, they sometimes don't live up to their values. Being honest about that, but also communicating a continued commitment to those values, can go a long way in building credibility. Leadership in a green company is an internal design component and is as important as what kind of roofing or paint you choose.

——— Building Your Company ——— for the Long Run

In his book, <u>Change Leaders</u>, management consultant, Peter Drucker, states: "One thing is certain: We face years of profound changes. It is futile to try to ignore the changes and to pretend that tomorrow will be like yesterday, only more so. . . . The changes are not predictable. The only policy likely to succeed . . . is to make the future."

Pulling Together Through Change

Focusing on your company's ability to change creates flexibility in how you do things. That built-in flexibility allows you not only to lead the market by building green, but it can help you deal with the ever-changing market itself. The economy has been good for an unprecedented length of time. But any builder who has been around for a few decades knows that building homes can be an economic roller-coaster ride. You have to be able to withstand the down times by knowing how to ride it out. A strong commitment to a corporate vision can help everyone get through the hard times together.

A case in point was my construction company, Lightworks Construction. We were committed to creating a culture that was employee-friendly. We spent a great deal of time creating an environment where employees felt that they had a role in the direction of the company and how it was managed, and that they shared in the profitability of the entire operation.

We created a corporate mission together. In developing the mission, we explored variations of management styles and job production and discussed the quality of buildings we wanted to build. Each month we had a town meeting with an outside facilitator to keep personal issues from building up and to improve open communication. Each field employee had experience in being a part of a crew. They built such trust, cooperation, and flow that every member of the crew knew exactly his/her job. The crew experience created a bond between them that was, at times, deeper than family. Laying a good foundation from the beginning gave us the strength to make things work over the long haul.

We made a significant investment in our people, knowing that replacement was difficult and expensive. We often "mixed it up" to give our crew the experience of working with different people. We trained young carpenters under different lead carpenters. This training increased their skill base and brought the team closer together. As a result, the guys spent a lot of time together both at work and after hours.

We experienced good times and tough times, as in all construction companies. When times were good we played together and celebrated our successes. When times were difficult we pulled together to figure out how to get through them. This was the real test of our corporate culture, because with tough times come fear and apprehension of the future. Human nature is such that fear often brings out self-interest over the collective good.

The greatest test was during the recession of the late '80s. The Washington, D.C., market was supposed to be recession-proof. The market had been hot for years and we had been able to build and grow as if there were no tomorrow…only tomorrow hit us like a ton of bricks falling from a scaffold. When the recession hit D.C., it was as though someone threw a circuit breaker, and the market just stopped. The recession-proof city took an economic dive, and construction was one of the hardest-hit sectors.

The only option we saw was to downsize, but we couldn't downsize fast enough. For the first time, we started losing money month after month. The overhead monster was nipping at our tails. It came to the point where we had to start laying off carpenters. It was a tough decision. We knew their wives and kids. We knew their dogs by name. We knew their life stories. These were friends, not just employees.

We went through the first round of layoffs with much anguish. There was a little fat in the company and that went first. When we got down to the real meat, the highly skilled carpenters, it became even more difficult. We called a town meeting and discussed our plight with the entire company. It was clear that there wasn't enough work for everyone and that a few field employees had to go or the company was going to go down. I asked the guys for input and suggestions.

Unbeknownst to us office guys, the field employees went to a bar after the meeting to discuss the situation. They sent a representative into the office the next day to tell us what they had decided. Rather than lay anybody else off, they each committed to take a 15 percent cut in wages. Their back of-the-napkin calculations the night before showed that they would save enough to keep everyone employed. We were blown away by the generosity of spirit behind the suggestion. We could only honor their wishes and keep everyone on board.

Over the next few months, they worked their tails off. They would come to the job on weekends to get ahead and not bill the company for the hours. They would salvage materials from one jobsite to augment another. They helped each other bring jobs in under budget so the surplus could keep the office staff employed. We produced like we never had before.

We made it through the worst of times by everyone pulling together and working as one mind and one heart. The company was more that a job: it was their life. And together they made it work.

The bottom line is that you are not just creating a sustainable green company, you are doing better business. And better business is not just getting the technical know-how you need; your real competitive advantage lies in your leadership and how well you work with your people.

Creating a Green Culture

Dennis Allen built some of the first solar homes in Santa Barbara. He sees a revival of solar in the marketplace and a burgeoning interest in green building. A group of architects, planners, city officials, interior designers, and Allen, the only builder, started the Sustainability Project in Santa Barbara. Allen Associates did most of the green projects in Santa Barbara. They never imposed it on clients, partners, or their supervisors, but they kept getting green work.

> **Dennis Allen**
> **Allen Associates, Santa Barbara**
> **(805) 682-4305**
> **www.silcom.com/-dallen/**
> *Dennis Allen is president of Allen and Associates, a 60-person construction firm that focuses mainly on high-end residential homes while doing some commercial building. Dennis got involved with solar energy in the mid-1970s, but it wasn't until 1999, that others in the company decided to make Allen Associates a green company, incorporating sustainable measures on all their projects. For the past two years they have won the Green Builder of the Year Award for their region and have had projects featured in national publications, including one especially innovative project that was on the cover of* Solar Age.

"During a business planning process with a consultant, the core group of company participants wanted to make the entire company green. It's quite a process to integrate new values into a company. Ten key employees started the process, with a retired VP of Gillette as facilitator. Then we held subsequent meetings with the partners and business manager," says Allen.

Re-Envisioning the Company

The process was not just about greening the company, but re-envisioning the company. To make the company consistent with the values identified by the core group, Allen Associates looked at how it conducted business across the board. This included starting a process of management by objectives. Once the company had identified its mission and objectives, each key staff member developed personal objectives to meet company objectives. Extra compensation and bonuses were tied to meeting the objectives.

Training Employees and Working With Trades

Allen trained junior employees and foremen in bimonthly sessions that included the specifics of green building, managing the trades, dealing with clients, and being more productive. In addition, Allen reached out to the trades and talked to them about how to make it work for them as well. This resulted in keeping costs in line, increased productivity, and other basic benefits to the trades companies.

In summary, to make the change to green values within your company:

- Start with your vision. Talk about it, get input on it, and invite your employees to think about the vision and add their ideas.

- Create a mission statement that will guide your decisions.

- When it comes time to actually implement the vision and mission, empower you employees to make decisions and take actions in line with the vision.

- Develop a strong team that will be flexible enough to pull through even the hard times.

Your employees, after all, are the ones who are "hands on," and they know the daily workings of the business well. Their buy-in and their expertise are key to implementing green changes.

Design

Design is a key element in creating a successful green home. And since design can have such an impact on the cost of the project, it is important to look closely at the entire design process. The American Institute of Architects has taken a strong position on sustainable design. Its Committee on the Environment (COTE) has become one of the leading organizations in the country promoting green building. Whether design is done in-house or by an architectural firm, an integrated design approach not only saves money in construction costs but creates a better, more integrated final product.

—— An Integrated Approach —— to Sustainable Design

An effective green building is a solution greater than the sum of its parts.

McStain Enterprises has included the following in their mission statement: "Design and build visionary communities that integrate the aesthetic, physical, and emotional needs of our customers." For McStain, a new home or development is always connected to the rest of the community.

Addressing transportation and utility infrastructure when siting homes, for example, can save the community money and ease the long-term burden of new development. Green buildings increase environmental sustainability and improve the quality of life when all the important issues are considered in concert with one another.

Successful green buildings are systems of integrated processes and products. A green building strives for the best integration of planning, sustainable actions, and technologies. This integrated approach increases the efficiency of the building and helps reduce overall costs by bringing together the experts in each of the systems early in the design process. But it can also be a challenge since building design is so often fragmented among the team of architects, builders, interior designers, mechanical contractors, and the trades.

—— Key Principles of —— Sustainable Design

The following principles have been heralded by the design community and have become the foundation for billion-dollar company CEOs like Ray Anderson of Interface Carpet of North Carolina. These principles can stimulate your thinking about sustainability as you consider the design of new projects. Even if you choose only two or three, you will be thinking in systems that will benefit your community

"Hannover Principles" or "Bill of Rights for the Planet"

Developed by William McDonough Architects of Charlottesville, Virginia.

1. Insist on the right of humanity and nature to coexist in a healthy, supportive, diverse, and sustainable condition.

2. Recognize interdependence. The elements of human design interact with and depend on the natural world, with broad and diverse implications at every scale. Expand design considerations to recognizing even distant effects.

3. Respect relationships between spirit and matter. Consider all aspects of human settlement including community, dwelling, industry, and trade in terms of existing and evolving connections between spiritual and material consciousness.

4. Accept responsibility for the consequences of design decisions upon human well-being, the viability of natural systems, and their right to coexist.

5. Create safe objects of long-term value. Do not burden future generations with requirements for maintenance or vigilant administration of potential danger due to the careless creation of products, processes, or standards.

6. Eliminate the concept of waste. Evaluate and optimize the full life cycle of products and processes, to approach the state of natural systems in which there is no waste.

7. Rely on natural energy flows. Human designs should, like the living world, derive their creative forces from perpetual solar income. Incorporate this energy efficiently and safely for responsible use.

8. Understand the limitations of design. No human creation lasts forever, and design does not solve all problems. Those who create and plan should practice humility in the face of nature. Treat nature as a model and mentor, not an inconvenience to be evaded or controlled.

9. Seek constant improvements by sharing knowledge. Encourage direct and open communication between colleagues, patrons, manufacturers, and users to link long-term sustainable considerations with ethical responsibility, and reestablish the integral relationship between natural processes and human activity.

—————— Phases of an Integrated —————— Design Process

Jim Van Derhyden of Investec uses an integrated design approach long before the project begins. Investec is building 147 units on the coast of California from Ventura County to San Luis Obispo County. San Luis Obispo and Santa Barbara are headed toward being no growth, and planners are concerned about what the next 25 years will do to the area.

About two years ago, Investec decided to be ahead of the curve in green building. As a developer, they came in with a very conscious plan and were flexible regarding the dictates of the powers that be. Through their green program they had a better chance at getting approvals than some of the other major builders. Their sustainable projects made them different. They knew that in the end green building was going to be one of the requirements of entitlement, that is, one of the requirements of the building process.

Van Derhyden explains their process for green design: "If you plan it right, you can build green at the same price as if it were a regular production home. We needed to get the architect on board by sitting down with him before we even started working with drawings."

They told the architect that they wanted the green concept to be in his mind before he designed the system. They went over every plan and determined where the heat exchanger would be and where the ducting would go. Every duct would be short and in conditioned space. They gave the architect rough schematics of every plan they wanted to do. Even before they got into the entitlement process for the land, they had gone through the whole system with him and everyone on the team so they could make efficient buildings. "In the end," Van Derhyden says, "we do a greener house for the same price as a conventional house by planning ahead for good systems."

The following section describes in detail the integrated aspects of a collaborative design process. This is one model of many that have been used by developers and builders across the country to incorporate green thinking early. Spending time up front and bringing everyone together to design a new project, as Van Derhyden and others have found, often keeps construction costs down and improves quality at the same time.

Phase 1 - Designing the Framework

Before any design process begins, establish a guiding framework. The framework helps the design team to understand the range of issues and decide on which to address through the course of the project. Taking this step minimizes the potential downside of making assumptions.

In this phase, define the decisions you want to make, the ends you want to achieve, and the means you will use to reach those ends. The most important point in this phase is for all parties who have decision-making responsibility to understand and support the goals and the means to achieving those goals.

Phase 2 - Assembling the Team

Key steps:

1. Structure the team to embrace the concept of "whole systems thinking," or integrated design. This process is different from traditional approaches because the design team includes the principals of all companies involved in designing and building the project. Every team member is encouraged to cross-fertilize the design with solutions to problems that may relate to, but are not typically addressed by their specialty. The objective of this phase is to have every member of the design team understand the issues that the other members need to address. This process produces more thorough and integrated solutions.

2. Involve the construction manager or superintendent in the design phase. The manager or super can offer immediate feedback about cost and construction issues, which can shorten debates on the merits of certain systems and materials over others. It also allows the superintendent to be an integral team member and to buy-in to the new concept early on. When people understand why they are important to a project, they are less resistant to new techniques. More often than not, a design is improved when the truly practical issues are considered up front.

3. Hire an environmental consultant to bring resources and experience to the table.

4. Include appropriate trade contractors, especially mechanical contractors, in the process.

5. Ask the marketing staff to participate.

When all participants in the project are involved, the design process is more efficient, resolves problems, and identifies potential cost savings early.

Phase 3 - Preparing Team Members for the Design Charrette

A "charrette" is a process in which the design team and related professionals assemble to establish a clear understanding about the project goals, analyze existing conditions, explore alternate solutions, and suggest or choose courses of action that are based on all the factors that may affect the final design. Before the design charrette takes place, though, certain issues need to be understood and organized so that when the design team meets, they can integrate concepts and solutions in the most time-efficient manner. This phase focuses on researching and analyzing:

- Local climate issues
- Energy loads—heating, cooling, lighting
- Other loads such as water, wastewater and storm water
- Availability of local materials and reclaimed building components
- Land issues—animal habitat, existing water courses, existing ecosystem
- Plant species that are available and appropriate in landscaping
- Traffic impacts on the surrounding community

COURTESY OF BARRETT-STEELE ARCHITECTS

From the above data, prepare an initial menu of ideas, priorities, and goals that can be accomplished and successfully marketed if incorporated into the project.

Phase 4 - The Charrette

Hold the charrette at a site where everyone can concentrate fully. Interruptions and phone calls drastically reduce efficiency and effectiveness. This process can take a full day or more. Find a site that has a room large enough to hold the design team as well as space for breakout groups.

The breakout groups will consist of a cross-section of the design team disciplines. Begin with the large group discussing general findings and approaches. Define the goals and issues for the breakout groups to analyze, such as siting and landscaping, energy issues, efficient use of materials, indoor air quality opportunities, marketability, etc. After a certain period, the breakout groups reassemble to present their approaches. Their ideas will be integrated or adapted into the overall plan.

COURTESY OF BARRETT-STEELE ARCHITECTS

The charrette can produce a number of things depending on the issues and the extent to which they can be resolved within the time frame. The objective is to come up with several potential design solutions for the team to analyze and evaluate. A final solution isn't necessarily produced, but the issues are explored and understood by all the participants involved in the project. Sharing information and mutual understanding are the most important products.

Phase 5 - Distilling the Results—Costs and Analysis

After the charrette, research and analyze your results with greater attention to detail. The planners, engineers, interior designers, trades contractors, specialists, and architects will take their respective issues and organize their optimal solutions. The cost estimator can determine a fairly accurate cost for the design at this stage.

COURTESY OF ENSAR GROUP

Phase 6 - Presentation and Review

The refined solution is presented to the reassembled design team for comment. If the team calls for significant changes, those changes will need to be redrawn. Minor changes can be verbally communicated and incorporated during the design development phase.

Phase 7 - Design Development

Design development requires more research and computer/drafting board time for the individual disciplines. During this phase, designers determine the exact material specifications, finishes, structural member sizes, and mechanical system equipment specifications. Designers produce accurately analyzed drawings. Performance criteria and costs are more refined at this stage.

Phase 8 - Construction Documents

This is traditionally the phase where all the design issues are organized into construction drawings and specifications.

Once the design is complete, it is presented to the company as the first step in creating a new green development or project. This is often conducted in a "town meeting" setting with some pomp and circumstance to create a sense of value around the introduction of the

COURTESY OF ENSAR GROUP

design. It is also a time to get the attention of the rest of the staff to encourage further buy-in.

Design is the inspiring side of the building business. Sometimes you see it as an end unto itself: "Look at what we've designed! Isn't it beautiful, and ain't we great?" But the execution is where it all becomes real. For great architecture to become a great building, it takes the cooperation and commitment from a lot of people as it grows from the ground up. The next section looks at working with construction employees and trades to make sure that projects go smoothly.

Aligning Employee Jobs with Green Building

One aspect of implementing the green vision and mission includes looking at each set of construction employees according to their responsibilities. These include procurement and estimating, field personnel, trades contractors, and the sales force. Each has an important role to play to ensure the success of the green program.

Estimating and Procurement

Resources need to be made available so that estimators and procurement staff can easily make green substitutions. If it is difficult to find and price green substitutions, they will likely choose products with which they are comfortable and familiar. The process of making green replacements involves research:

- Who has the products?
- What do they cost?
- Are prices competitive?
- Are the products in stock or readily available?
- Do you have an account with the supplier?
- Does the supplier have a good reputation in the industry?

The *Environmental Building News Product Catalog* is a great single source for most green products. (See Appendix B for source.)

Making green changes often results in creating new relationships with new suppliers. If you want to keep your current suppliers, work with them to handle new lines. If you commit to a new product line, such as finger-jointed studs, for instance, the local lumberyard may be willing to carry them as long as they know you will buy them.

For example, five years ago I specified finger-jointed studs for a green home I was working on. I researched their availability. No one in the Denver metro market carried them. The lumberyard the builder used said they would be happy to handle the studs if I could prove a demand for a rail carload of them. That was a lot of houses, and the builder wouldn't commit to that many of anything!

Through the HBA environmental committee, I asked members if any of them were interested in committing to finger-jointed studs. Several builders said that if I could get the price right they would use them. I called the manufacturer and told him we were seeding the market for their product and asked if he would adjust the price on less than a carload. He did. I brought the price (which was close to solid-sawn 2x4 prices) to the lumberyard. The owner agreed to carry the studs. Since that time, the finger-jointed studs have been as available to us as regular studs—and they are much straighter!

Superintendents

Because the supers' attitude about the change will affect the attitude of the other workers, they are where "rubber meets the road." The field mentality is generally different from that of the office crew. The best intentions in your plans can fall apart in the race for expediency. Supers have two primary motivations: Get the job done on time, and bring it in under budget. Beyond that, they consider many of the directives from the office as "their problem."

Tom Hoyt says, "Construction superintendents may not support what you are doing, but if you can paint the picture for them of what the advantages are and get their input, they will tell you where the problems will be. If you don't listen to them, that's where you can really get screwed up. You need to use them, and that's part of how you get their buy-in."

If supers think they are part of designing a more efficient framing system, they are less likely to throw in that other 2x4 that isn't needed. And they are less likely to install a new material incorrectly because they don't believe in it to begin with. You have to educate them about the advantages of the products and how to install them. Involve them in deciding which green products to use, and take the time to train them well.

➔ To succeed with supers, ensure that all green changes are seen as being in the best interest of those in the field. For example, indoor air quality (IAQ) is typically targeted at homeowners and their kids. But many major impacts of IAQ are most acute when the products are being installed. The health of field personnel can be jeopardized as they spray solvent-based finishes or use toxic adhesives in a closed space.

Kristin Shewfelt of McStain says, "Building green requires a shift in thinking throughout the entire company. For example, our green building checklist stated that we use mastic on all our ductwork. But lo and behold, I was walking around a site one day and saw that we were using duct tape. We were using mastic on the main plenum duct, but we were still wrapping the other feeds and returns with duct tape. I went to our superintendent and said, 'What's the big deal?' And he said, 'Well, our mechanical contractor wants to charge two hundred dollars extra a home for that.' I called up the contractor and said, 'What will you charge on a 2,000 sq. ft. home to mastic it all?' And he quoted me about a hundred fifty dollars. The super evidently threw off some figure that would discourage me from pursuing it further. But I pursued it further and recommended that we consider mastic throughout."

Shewfelt continued to say that Max Sherman from the Laurence Berkeley Laboratories in California did an age study test on duct tape, UL81 rated foil-backed tape, and mastic. Duct tape failed miserably in the aging test. Some of the foil-backed tapes performed a lot better and so were good alternatives to duct tape. But his strong recommendation was that when given the choice, go to mastic. "It wasn't until we started getting those studies that construction personnel were finally willing to consider an alternative," she said.

——— Involving Your ———
Trade Contractors

Imagine a graph with the building industry in the center. Around its periphery are vendors, trade contractors, and businesses, each with their own economic needs and structures. They have to learn to build in relation to one another so that they are all supportive of one another. Yet typically, each tends to act very independently.

I have often run into the difficulty of getting the trade contractors on board when working on the first green home for a builder. From this experience, I learned how important it is to get them

all together before the job starts. The following story is an example of working with a trade person who has never used green products:

I was brought in to work on a model home in a new sub-division. The home was to exemplify all the green features the builder wanted to incorporate into the development. It was a design/build firm, so we had control over both the design and construction from start to finish. We had many meetings to ensure that all the field employees and subs knew the new routine and were on board. It was a great project, and most of the crew bought in and enjoyed the process.

We were on schedule to be open for a gala event that had been planned for months. One Saturday, I got a call from the builder. He was having trouble with his painter. The painter had used the same supplier for 20 years and refused to use the new VOC-free paint that I had specified. He said he knew the performance of the paint he had always used and wouldn't warranty the new paint. He was sure it would fail or peel or not cover well. Therefore, since he had worked with the builder for years, he wouldn't install an inferior product.

The builder was at his wit's end and asked if I would talk to the painter and try to convince him to get with the program. I called him. We talked and talked, and reluctantly he agreed to use the new paint.

On the second day of spraying, I stopped by the job to see how it was going. I was walking through the house when I heard someone yell, "Hey you! Are you that green guy? " I yelled back, "Yeah, what can I do for you?" "Let's step out to the garage, we need to talk," he said, taking off his dust mask. I was sure I was about to get an earful.

He looked like a ghost with a nose and mouth. The rest of him was covered with back spray. He was a big guy and I wasn't sure what to expect. He looked at me and said, "You know, all along I felt your were full of ____! I've been painting for 20 years and know my business. But last night something odd happened. Usually, I come home from work exhausted, take a nap, wake up just in time to say good night to my kids and eat some cold dinner. I get ready for the next day and they go to bed. It's been a pattern for years. Last night when I got home I felt great! I played with the kids, had dinner with the family, and did some bookwork before bed. Today I feel like a million bucks. I just wanted to thank you for introducing me to this new stuff. I had no idea how much normal paint was taking out of me and affecting my life!"

Vernon McKown has a process for integrating trade contractors into his company. "We believe in trade partnering," McKown says. "It's a cultural issue with us. We have always been big at treating the trades with respect and dignity. We treat them like business owners. Teach them how to do good business. You can't just tell the subs to build green."

McKown holds trade meetings each quarter and asks what their issues are. He wants to know what the company can do to reduce problems and help the trades make more money. Framing crews, for example, are small businesses, typically two to five guys. Getting paid on time is the most important thing to them.

"We pay subs every 36 hours," McKown says. "We are the fastest-paying general contractor in the state. We go back to the basics. If we

Vernon McKown, Ideal Homes
Norman, Oklahoma
(800) 682-2763
www.ideal-homes.com
Vernon McKown is president of Ideal Homes, the largest production builder in Oklahoma. They build four hundred homes each year in the $60,000 - $130,000 range, which are aimed at first time buyers. Ideal Homes has also built an American Lung Association Health House.

meet their biggest needs, they will reciprocate. They are extremely amenable. We have had no problems with their participation. They are partnering with us in our 'productive quality' program."

➲ You have to get the trade relationship going before you can get green building going. When you look at the trades, builders are always asking them to do more: higher quality, faster, cheaper. Identify their needs before you ask them to meet yours, McKown suggests.

Trade relationships are complicated and have often been in place for many years. It is especially difficult when the change to green building requires bringing in a new contractor for an aspect of the job that the old one isn't qualified for.

"At McStain we've made great strides in involving our vendors in our building practices and asking for their help in constant improvement," Shewfelt says.

McStain still sees places where building practices are entrenched, though, because relationships are entrenched. For instance, Shewfelt says, "Joe Shmoe has been working with Bubba, the foundation guy, for years, and they bowl together on Saturday nights. If Bubba isn't willing to change, Joe will have to use a different foundation company. This could be a difficult decision for him to make. Integrating green building practices with the peripheral venders, subcontractors, and businesses can require reestablishing and restructuring relationships. That's part of the challenge for a lot of green building companies."

➲ Working with the trades can be your key to success. As with any relationship, when they know you are concerned with their bottom line, they will be there when you need them and will bend over backwards to help create the best job they can. When demand for trade contractors is high and they can pick and choose who they work for, it is just good business to treat them well and let them know you expect their best.

—————— Sales and Marketing Team ——————

Your sales team or the realtors you use present your face to the customer. How they represent you and your homes is the most important element in selling your product. You typically have one chance with a buyer. They will rarely come back if they don't get a good impression. You can build the best green home in town, but if your sales people don't see the value in the green features, they won't represent you or the home appropriately to the customer.

COURTESY OF ENSAR GROUP

Tom Hoyt says, "The sales staff needs to believe that what you are doing is going to make it easier for them to sell homes." McStain has seen its sales staff ignore a green program because they didn't understand it or didn't believe they were giving their customers value. Although they had an effective tool in differentiating the green product from someone else's, they didn't have confidence in it, so they didn't use it. "I've seen that half a dozen times or more here," Hoyt says. "That's why their buy-in is so critical."

Companies that successfully "sell green in a black and white world" show their sales people that they can make more money and bring buyers back through understanding the benefits of green building. We started this book by saying that building green is more about people than about technology. Green gives sales people tools to engage the buyer on an emotional level. When they believe that there are greater benefits to the buyer of a green home over a conventional home, their belief and enthusiasm can close the sale by itself.

A company aligned to a mission that is greater than the bottom line is an attractive force to be reckoned with. It creates a magic that businesses in the black and white world can't imagine. Prospective employees often come to you because of your reputation as a great place to work.

Customers feel it. They are confident doing business with you when they hear the same commitment to quality, people, and the environment from every member of the team they encounter. Finding a company with integrity and a higher purpose is something most people are longing for. When you can take that step and inspire those who work for you to join with you, there is no competition. Everyone else is measured against your standard.

Marketing Strategies

5

This chapter gives you specific information on how to market green. Marketing benefits—not the features—sells homes. Working in the best interests of the whole community helps develop sales allies. Each section includes examples of what has worked for other builders.

Community Relations - Unwanted growth and urban sprawl is often blamed on builders. Incorporating green features into homes and developments is a good way to improve a builder's image in the community.

Media Relations - Green building is newsworthy. Getting the news media on your doorstep is the trick.

Brochures - Seeing is believing! Brochures offer a chance to display photos of your past jobs and allow you to express intangibles such as your company's values.

Marketing Strategies - Learn key questions to ask as you decide how to approach your market.

Marketing Green in a Black and White World is an opportunity to reinvent the relationship of your company with your community. You are making a statement that you have a commitment to something greater than the bottom line. You care about the impact of your homes and are willing to publicly put your values in front of your potential market. Not only can you change the way your community views your work, but you can help change the perspective that builders don't care about anything but selling more homes.

> *"I don't think you can market green buildings, I think you have to market the benefits of green buildings. Buyers make decisions based on benefits, no matter what they're purchasing. You've got to figure out what the need of that buyer is. Whether you are in the business of building custom homes or a development, customers are not buying the home, they are buying the benefits."*
>
> *—John Knott, Developer and CEO of Dewees Island, South Carolina.*

Marketing green is an opportunity to conduct a promotional campaign in unique and fun ways. By setting yourself and your company apart from the other builders in your area, you step into a new world of recognition and media attention. Your homes draw the public's curiosity and interest, and you have a story to tell that is attractive to the media. By thinking outside of the traditional marketing box you can engage more of the public than you may have thought possible. People start to remember the name of your company as the builder who cares. Many builders have pursued this image through involving their company in community activities. Some have taken leadership positions within their local building industry associations using green building to enhance their careers.

This chapter explores a variety of marketing approaches that have proven successful for builders across the country. There are few renown marketing gurus in the home building business, but several people have risen to the top because of their creativity and sales success. Whether it is through politics, or just throwing the best party in town, these approaches have brought recognition, referrals, and return customers to their businesses.

Community Relations

Building green is a great way to redefine the role of homebuilders in the community. Pressures of growth are creating traffic congestion, crowded schools, and long lines at favorite restaurants, and builders are taking the brunt of the blame. Many people feel that growth is unchecked and that it reduces the quality of life in their communities. Open space, parks, and bike trails are aspects of green building that counter complaints that we are paving over paradise. Addressing environmental issues head-on and demonstrating how green building helps to alleviate environmental problems can take a homebuilder from being the culprit to being a community leader.

The building industry, through green building programs, is one of the few large industries to make a visible effort to reduce the environmental impact of their business. Through building green, community leadership roles are available to builders who want to take a public stand.

John Abrams, president of South Mountain Company, Inc., shares his thoughts on community relations:

John Abrams
South Mountain Company, Inc.
Martha's Vineyard, Massachusetts
(508) 693-4850
www.somoco.com
South Mountain Company is an employee owned design/build firm that does development, architecture, and building. SMC's work includes custom new homes and renovations, affordable housing and cohousing projects, and occasional commercial and institutional projects.

"We are very active in the community. We don't advertise. All of our work comes from word of mouth. Our reputation brings in all of our new work. People see we are involved in civic and political work and get to know us. We are active in affordable housing advocacy, renewable energy advocacy, transportation issues, and we are helping to chart a course for a more sustainable island. Five percent of our profits go to local charity. Those who believe in what we do come to us as a result." Although most builders will need to supplement their community relations with other means of reaching prospective buyers, John Abrams' story reflects how crucial community involvement can be to bringing in new business.

Since protecting the environment is increasingly becoming a core American value, expressing environmental concern translates into popularity in political arenas. As a result, local political leaders often welcome being associated with green builders in order to be in the media spotlight. In Colorado, both the governor and the mayor of Denver have made cameo appearances and public endorsements of the Colorado HBA Built Green Program. By involving political leaders in

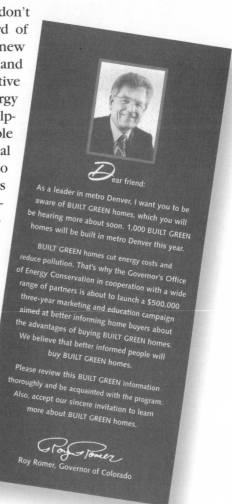

Dear friend:

As a leader in metro Denver, I want you to be aware of BUILT GREEN homes, which you will be hearing more about soon. 1,000 BUILT GREEN homes will be built in metro Denver this year.

BUILT GREEN homes cut energy costs and reduce pollution. That's why the Governor's Office of Energy Conservation in cooperation with a wide range of partners is about to launch a $500,000 three-year marketing and education campaign aimed at better informing home buyers about the advantages of buying BUILT GREEN homes. We believe that better informed people will buy BUILT GREEN homes.

Please review this BUILT GREEN information thoroughly and be acquainted with the program. Also, accept our sincere invitation to learn more about BUILT GREEN homes.

Roy Romer, Governor of Colorado

your promotions, you gain recognition as a credible green builder and as someone dedicated to improving the community. As an old politician once said, "Show me a parade, and I'll gladly get in front of it!"

Media Relations

Mon., April 22, 1996   Rocky Mountain News

Building industry going green

By Paul MacGregor
Special to the News

A growing number of products that used to clog landfills are showing up as building and decorating materials in new homes and remodeling projects at an increasing rate.

lic's environmental consciousness grows, the materials add to homes' attractiveness and salability.

The demand for the products has spawned manufacturing firms and building-supply dealers that specialize in recycled building materials. Alex Wilson, who publish-

use in decks.

Murphy predicts that his product and that of competitors, Trex and CareFree, will account for more than 10% of deck and other outdoor lumber uses in the United States over the next decade.

For years, Denver companies such as Architectural Salvage

The local media can be your best marketing ally. Green building is press worthy. Another new subdivision or building project is not very exciting to news reporters, but a new home that is good for the environment and healthier for children has many angles for a reporter to use as a "hook."

Green building stories can show up in many parts of the newspaper other than the real estate section. Building green is business news and is often featured prominently to highlight a new business approach. Environmental stories can show up in the science section by covering a specific aspect of green building such as indoor air quality or saving trees. Local news sections are always looking for features that highlight a local business. You want to get your story into as many hands as possible. Often other sections of the paper will reach your prospective buyers more effectively than the real estate section.

Peter Pfeiffer, an Austin, Texas, architect involved in sustainable architecture, says, "I realized that contributing articles to professional journals is

Fine Homebuilding

Squaring Mudsills   •   Looking at Windows   •   Steel-Stud Remodeling

September 1995 No. 97
U.S. $5.95, U.K. £3.00, Canada $6.95

Building a 'Green' House

Fine Homebuilding

nice, but publications like *Better Homes and Gardens* main-stream green. They are some of the best marketing approaches we have done. I get fifty times the response from these articles than I get from a professional magazine. The same is true for the papers. When I can get into a section other than real estate, I get a much better response."

—— Attracting the Media ——

Creating public events at the home site is an effective way to attract media attention. Philip Russell in Pensacola, Florida, conducts special classes for school children at their new homes before they hang the sheet rock. This program is called the Behind the Walls Expo™. School buses line the streets, and television cameras are close by to feature the little ones learning about the environment in a new home. At one such event, the local TV stations covered the event with generous airtime. This TV coverage drew in long lines of prospective home-buyers and the home was sold the next week. (See the case study in Chapter 7.)

—— Target Your Advertising Carefully ——

Bill Eich, a builder in northern Iowa, learned the value of marketing green and dramatically grew his business through advertising. Local advertising didn't result in much sales activity so he ran his ads in a regional magazine that featured his homes in the "lake country." The magazine's circulation covered a wider area and attracted retirement and second home-buyers from around the region. All of his ads show Eich putting the kick plate on after final inspection, his personal signature of quality.

The kickplate is the last thing we ever do.

Long before I put the kickplate on your door, I'll help make sure your new home is perfectly designed ... to fulfill your family's dreams

Brochures

Your brochure is often your first chance to present who you are to your buyers. You can communicate a lot in a brochure through a good description of your corporate values, your approach to building, and the ways you show that you care about your clients. Just seeing your homes doesn't necessarily give potential buyers an opportunity to hear about those issues. For

example, a builder named Doug Parker wanted to let his community know that he was a different kind of builder. He had been building in Boulder, Colorado, based on his reputation of 25 years. Most of his jobs were referrals. This provided a relatively steady, if not particularly satisfying, stream of job opportunities. Yet, he longed for a new set of job prospects that would be more challenging and more consistent with the direction he wanted the company to go.

Doug hired Standing Stone Design of Boulder, Colorado, to create a new image for his company, Big Horn Builders. His previous presentation package was based on snapshots of past jobs in a haphazard portfolio. Since he had been referred by past clients, he had personal references that helped build his clients' confidence, but the only way he could truly show what he had done was to take prospective clients on a house tour of past jobs. This was often inconvenient and difficult to schedule. Standing Stone suggested he display a montage of past work in a unique brochure so he could emphasize the quality of his work and his commitment to energy efficiency and green products. The result is shown on the previous page.

Doug increased his exposure by being the only green builder on the Tour of Homes. He displayed a wonderful example of green design and labeled each of the features with wall plaques describing their benefits. There had never been a Tour home with that kind of detailed explanation of green features. The public was fascinated with the educational component that went beyond pretty kitchens and expansive master suites. Doug's brochure let them know that Big Horn Builders was both a quality builder and environmentally conscious. He jumped to another level in the market based on that approach and has become known as the green remodeler in Boulder.

Doug took his prominence in the market and grew it into a part time consulting business with the City of Boulder, training other builders in how to build green. His recognition also got the attention of the local HBA, which invited him to sit on their board of directors.

Other builders have experienced similar success based on telling their green story. The combination of compelling graphic design and depiction of green products typically hidden behind the walls make the benefits of the home for the buyer a very effective sales tool.

McStain Enterprises effectively uses brochures and sales materials to communicate their green building ethic. Their Greenlee Park brochure identifies the why and how of green building to prospective buyers. The brochure is backed up by a well-trained sales team that gives tours of homes, showing the features identified in the brochure.

Marketing Strategies

Marketing is the process of getting your customer through the door. It is the "make it or break it" component of business today. Good business is a lot more than building a good product at a reasonable price. You have to be different and better than the competition in order to get buyers' attention. That means you can't rely on the real estate section in the local paper alone. You have to look for unusual opportunities to get your message out to the public.

Vernon McKown, the largest builder in Oklahoma, says, "You have to be creative in your marketing. You don't have to be the greenest builder in America. You just have to be greener than the competition. Start with the greatest point of difference. Give it 24 months. The competition will follow, then you have to start something new. By 36 months everyone will be doing it.

"Our sales grew faster than average based on the quality of our homes. We saw a 65 percent increase in our sales last year, while building permits were only up 20 percent." The key to cornering the market is to be one of the first to make the switch, then you will always be a step ahead of your competition.

Marketing Green in a Black and White World means that you are not only building quality green homes, but you are marketing more creatively than your competition, who are building and marketing in traditional ways. You are cornering a market by finding new avenues to reach your buyers and creating a positive community-minded image of your company.

———— The Basics of a Good ———— Marketing Plan

For an excellent reference on developing a good marketing plan, refer to the book published by Home Builder Press called *Marketing New Homes*, written by David F. Parker and Charles R.

Clark. Parker and Clark identify the three M's of marketing as Manage, Market, and Monitor. They also provide a checklist of marketing activities that fall under each subheading.

Manage

The manage portion of marketing is focused on developing a marketing plan. Here are key steps:

Conduct Market Research. This important topic was discussed in chapter one. Market research provides you with facts about your most likely consumers, their preferences, the needs of their lifestyles, and what they are willing to pay for green features.

Get Market Information on Your Competition. Are they are using green to market their homes? Where are their strengths? Knowing this information will augment your own instincts about what the market needs and wants.

Manage
- *Market Research*
- *Consumer characteristics*
- *What are their needs?*
- *What are their preferences?*
- *What is their financial status?*
- *What is their interest in green?*
- *Product Definition*
- *Home type*
- *Design*
- *Pricing*
- *Benefits*
- *Features*
- *Marketing Plan/ Budget*
- *How to attract customers*
- *Costs associated with plan*
- *Marketing team*

Define Your Product. The combination of facts and intuition will guide you in deciding which green features to focus on in your homes and developments and let you know which consumer groups to target with various green packages.

Develop Your Marketing Plan. The first two steps of market research and product definition lay the groundwork for developing the actual marketing plan and budget. This plan aligns your promotional activities with your budget. Such a plan should take into account the sale of your entire development or span at least a year for multi-site builders.

Develop Your Marketing Team. The final step in managing your marketing plan is managing your marketing team. Your marketing team includes your staff along with outside consultants. Determine which roles people on your staff can fill and which roles need to be filled by outside consultants. Also, develop criteria to determine who will perform specific functions such as public relations, advertising, and educating community members on green building issues.

Coordinate Your Team. Create systems of communication and policies that will promote the coordination of your team.

Market

The market phase implements all the research and planning done in the manage phase. Choose your marketing objectives. Then determine the actions and team responsibilities for meeting them.

➲ **Create Your Green Market Identity.** One of the first steps of actively marketing is identity creation. Choose a name, a logo, and possibly a tag line—perhaps your mission statement—that will appear on all your stationery, advertisements, brochures, etc. Make sure your commitment to the environment is an integral part of the identity you are creating. This may mean changing your previous logo or mission statement. Use this change as an opportunity to communicate that it is not just your logo that is changing, but that your whole company is inherently different because you are choosing to build green.

➲ **Develop a Public Relations Strategy.** Public Relations is a key component in marketing. It is far more cost-effective than advertising and brings the credibility of the media that is covering you. Public relations involves finding ways to both inform and involve the public in what you are doing. Present your choice to build green as a choice to promote the well being of the community. Plan events that will enhance your image with consumers, local government, business executives, and real estate agents.

➲ **Advertise.** And of course, you will want to advertise. The key to advertising is discovering the most cost-effective method. As Chapter 1 explained, those most likely to be interested in green homes don't watch a lot of television; so you probably want to look into other options such as radio and print. Formulate a creative strategy to promote the benefits of green homes.

➲ **Merchandising Your Homes.** The last step in the market phase is merchandising. Merchandising is all about presentation. From the time the customer first enters the development sales office or the home, until the time they leave, every aspect–from landscaping to identification signs to the interior and exterior of the information center—should focus on creating a desire in the customer to live there. Green building, however, can put a positive spin on this typical approach. Since most green features are not visible when the home is complete, part of your merchandising could include opening the home to prospective

Market
- *Identity Creation*
- *Names*
- *Logos*
- *Colors*
- *Collateral materials*
- *Public Relations*
- *Publicity*
- *Direct communications*
- *Community involvement*
- *Promotions*
- *Advertising*
- *Communications media*
- *Merchandising*
- *Model homes*
- *Information center*
- *Signage*
- *Interior design*

buyers while it is still under construction. Another option is to have green product samples and displays visible in the office. Also, while the home is being shown, a great merchandising technique is to label and explain the green features with signage to highlight the features.

Monitor

Monitoring brings this marketing approach full circle by analyzing the success of the marketing phase and making suggestions for the next management phase.

Get Consumer Feedback. To evaluate the success of your marketing get consumer opinions. You can gather this information easily by engaging prospective buyers in conversation as they tour your homes. Or they can fill out surveys which ask for their feedback on the home, as well as, what they consider to be pressing residential environmental concerns.

Monitor
- *Consumer opinions*
- *Primary market research*
- *Business improvement*
- *Competitive traits*
- *Other builders' offerings*
- *Performance evaluation*
- *Construction quality*
- *Performance of products*
- *Marketing*
- *Sales procedures*
- *Constant Improvement*
- *Revise your approach*
- *Train your sales team*
- *Upgrade your green features*
- *Ask:"What can we do better?"*

Keep an Eye on the Competition. Stay updated on the competitive traits of other builders. As you lead the way in green building, others are likely to follow suit. If you stay abreast of the green features and sales approaches your competition is using, you can more easily differentiate your homes. Your sales representatives can gather this information by using forms provided by a market research consulting service.

Evaluate Your Progress. Another element of the monitor phase, which is particularly important for green building, is performance evaluation. Since green building often uses many innovative products, it is crucial to go back and check the products' performance. You want to offer your homebuyers products that are not only healthy for the environment, but also of high quality and value to the buyer. Also, get continual feedback from your sales representatives on the effectiveness of your marketing and sales approach. Hold sales meetings regularly to evaluate what works and to strategize with your team on developing effective and creative marketing plans.

Modify Your Plan. Finally, all this information should result in modification and improvement of your original management plan.

Green marketing can enhance all of the steps listed in the sidebars. The section in Chapter 1 regarding doing your own market research, offers guidelines on answering the questions under the "manage" section. But the simplest advice for finding out what your customers want is to ask them. Product definition is deciding what approach to green building will be most successful in your market.

The end of this chapter gives some examples of how to combine green features to enhance overall benefit.

——— Develop an Innovative ——— Marketing Strategy

The marketing plan is where your creativity really starts. Now that you know who your buyers are, how do you get to them? Here are some examples that have been successful for other builders. Use these approaches; combine them; experiment until you find what works for you.

How will you define your product offering in relation to your market?

- *Energy efficiency?*
- *Solar energy?*
- *Indoor air quality?*
- *Saving old growth trees?*

• **Work with the local utility to jointly inform their customers that new alternatives in energy conserving homes are available.**

For example, the Good Cents Environmental Home Program has its roots in the Good Cents™ Program started by Southern Electric International, an electric utility that services Georgia, Alabama, Mississippi, and Florida. The Good Cents™ Program has certified 650,000 homes for energy efficiency since 1982. In 1994, the Environmental Home Program started working with utilities across the country. The Environmental Home Program assists builders in their service territory with marketing and media support. The program currently has utility

AT HOME WITH THE ENVIRONMENT

Throughout Nature, homes work in harmony with the environment. A bird builds its nest of gathered twigs. Bees collect pollen and nectar, transforming them into elaborate hives. A beaver uses branches from nearby trees. Each home is suited to its inhabitant, yet exists without upsetting the balance of Nature. Except homes built by man. Today's average new home can consume enough lumber to level an acre of timberland. It can generate up to four tons of waste during construction. It can use ___ technologies that waste energy or water. • Unless it is a Good Cents ___ Environmental Home. • You see, while Good Cents Environmental ___ Homes may look and feel like other new homes, they are built ___ with a commitment to give you more than the quality home you've ___ always wanted. Good Cents Environmental Homes take into ___ consideration the impact each part of the building process has on the environment. • Materials used in an Environmental Home are reviewed to determine which offer the best quality and durability without damaging the world. Building techniques are examined to see how well they suit the local terrain and climate. Energy efficiency and water conservation strategies are incorporated. In fact, over 500 areas are examined and rated. The higher the rating, the more environmentally friendly your home is.

partners in Alabama, Arizona, Georgia, Louisiana, Florida, Mississippi, New Jersey, New York, North Carolina, Oklahoma, Oregon, South Carolina, and Texas.

Training is available through the program, and the homes are certified using a computer program that weights the environmental features of the home. This rating provides the builder with a score he can use in his sales process. Their marketing support and brochures are some of the best and most beautiful on the market.

One of their builders, Bob Moore, was part of a development called Reynolds Plantation, outside of Atlanta. He built a green demonstration home as one of four open homes at the

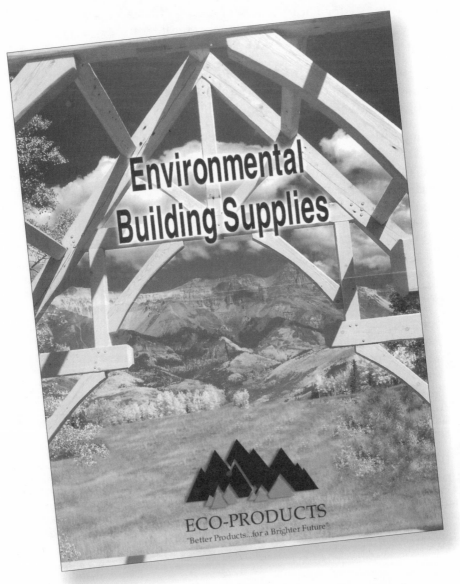

CATALOG COVER PHOTO BY PHILIP WEGENER KANTOR

development. On the opening day of the home showcase, he sold his home on the spot. Because of the green features in the home, and with the support of The Good Cents™ Program, during the month the homes were open, he sold six additional homes before any of the other builders sold their models.

• Work with your product manufacturers and their suppliers to create high visibility for your homes.

Your vendors, suppliers, and manufacturers of green products can be some of your greatest allies. They have a vested interest in your success. If you build green homes, and are successful at it, you will be buying more of their products. They also probably have a bigger marketing budget than you do.

Many builders across the country have used their suppliers as marketing allies. The most basic level is to do cooperative advertising. This works in many forms of media. Print ads displaying the logo of your major suppliers, radio spots that include their names or product lines, and TV commercials showing their products, can be prominently displayed in a show home. Often several non-competing suppliers can be included in the commercial.

The Denver Metro HBA Built Green program has taken full advantage of cooperative marketing. For the month before the Green Parade of Homes, the program assembled both builders and suppliers to contribute to a TV ad campaign. They were able to raise several hundred thousand dollars to flood the market with ads for the parade and for the builders participating.

Taking it to the next level, get your suppliers to become sponsors of your project. One of the best examples is the Energy Smart Program in Pensacola, Florida. Builder Philip Russell, as an example, stops construction before drywall is installed and opens the home to the public for the Behind-the-Walls Expo. It has proven to be a very successful marketing strategy.

The demonstration home is made possible by contributions from a "family of sponsors." Most sponsors participate because they find demonstrable value in the public exposure to their products. Russell's approach has drawn 60 sponsors who have contributed to the success of the Energy Smart™ Behind the Walls Expo including: Amoco, Pella, GE, Trus Joist MacMillan, IBM, Sears, OCF, Honeywell, and Carrier. "It's a real win-

win opportunity. Anytime we can find a true win-win we'll be right there," says Bill McNeal of J.F. Day, the regional distributor for Pella windows. "I'm working on weekends for no pay and no commissions because it's such a good marketing opportunity. I know it will generate future sales."

Sponsoring manufacturers offered seminars to contractors, plumbers, electricians, and carpenters in the appropriate use of their products. Art Southerland from Trus Joist MacMillan taught a course for builders. He says, "Our product, engineered floor joists, is not exposed in a finished home. The Behind the Walls Expo gives us visibility in a unique setting. The environmental focus is important to us. Our mission statement says that we will use no old growth timber in our product. This gives us a chance to get that message across." (See case study in Chapter 7.)

Other builders have worked successfully with their suppliers as well. When McStain built their Greenlee Park development of 180 homes, they invited their suppliers to contribute to their "green building museum." They filled one of the early open homes near the sales office with exhibits and displays for over 40 suppliers of products used in the development. These exhibits were left open to the public for a year. As buyers were introduced to the benefits of green features in the sales office, they were given tours of the products used in the show home. Greenlee Park was one of the most successful developments in the county at the time, in part due to its unique sales approach.

• **Work with the local chamber of commerce and hold VIP lunches in the new green model home. Invite civic and industry leaders to a guided tour that showcases all the environmental features and benefits to the community.**

At the McStain Greenlee Park development, the VIP event was intended to introduce the concept of green building to the significant people in McStain's business world. The event was conducted in cooperation with the Chamber of Commerce. A catered lunch was served to the assembled county commissioners, city council members, interested business owners, and community leaders. The intent was to associate McStain with affordable, energy efficient, environmentally sensitive development. The concept was that since there was pressure to restrict building in the county, those buildings which were approved should have a net positive benefit to the county and the municipalities. These were not just houses, they represented the state-of-the-art in environmentally-friendly housing. They were more affordable; they had less impact on local infrastructure through energy and water conservation features. They reduced the export of local dollars since less money was flowing out to distant power plants due to the increased energy efficiency of the homes. They were more politically correct (which all the politicians took credit for); and they represented a far-sighted view of development in the county.

The media was invited after lunch and participated in the tours of the environmental aspects of the homes. The event was a success. Subsequent McStain development in the county was facilitated by this early introduction of green features to the county officials. (See case study in Chapter 7.)

• **Have an "after hours" party for the neighborhood to show off the new product.**

Wildview was a new development that encompassed a wetland area in northern Colorado. The development took advantage of the lake area. Preserving the environment and wildlife habitat became the theme of the development.

Architect and builder Randy Hartman's project was the first green home to be built at Wildview. To market the home, Hartman created an event that made the home and the experience memorable. He called it "Cinco de Mayo Minus One" (May 4). He hired a mariachi band and created a dancing space. The event was

catered by one of the best restaurants in the area. Hartman partnered with a wildlife protection organization, in keeping with the theme of the development, and had eagle and hawk demonstrations on the patio. Guests were taken to the model home in horse-drawn wagons that circled around the parking area. An educational slide show was presented in the basement showing the house in all phases of construction, highlighting the green features. Before the event, Hartman courted local media. As a result, a video crew covered the event, which was a smashing success. Hartman sold the home. In fact, he felt he sold the home too soon. There was so much interest in it that he thought he could have sold it for a premium.

- **Create joint fundraising/marketing events with local environmental groups who share common interests.**

My construction company, Lightworks, specialized in co-marketing with other companies and organizations. One example that was highly successful was a result of research where we identified a target audience that was likely to use our design/build services. A friend was a salesman at a BMW dealer. We saw that we shared our perfect client in terms of demographics and decided to do a co-marketing event together. It was to be at his dealership. We invited an art gallery to join in the event and hired the tastiest caterer in town. To broaden the theme, we invited a solar energy non-profit organization to put up a display. We also made the event a fundraiser for the local symphony, which supplied a string quartet. We pooled our mailing lists, and several hundred people attended. Everyone involved felt the event was highly successful. It led to several high-end projects for us (I think it sold more Beemers though).

- **Send your staff to local schools to participate in green building seminars.**

Local schools are always looking for interesting new ways to augment their academic programs. Green building is a great way to bring together many of the topics that children are studying in school. Recycling home waste into building materials is a topic that always holds their attention. Environmental issues like global climate change and depletion of the ozone layer are typically covered in middle schools, and the role of buildings in reducing these issues is fascinating to these students. There are many opportunities to discuss what you are doing.

• Hold a green design competition at local high schools.

High school drafting and design classes appreciate having "real world" applications for their students. Each semester, I teach a class at a local high school. This is often done in conjunction with a local builder who offers $25-100 scholarship awards for the best green design. The competition is conducted with the support of a local newspaper or other media. This project educates young people and provides publicity for the students, the school, and the builder.

• Write an article on your projects for local newspapers.

Consider becoming a columnist for your local paper. If you live in a large metropolitan area, you might try one of the small local weekly newspapers first. They are particularly hungry for local news and features. I started my writing career by creating articles for a local paper. By being a columnist you can help to educate prospective home buyers about the features of green building that are most important in your market. This, in turn, will make your sales process easier. Also, when you contribute to the paper, they will be more likely to cover you as a news feature as well. This writing experience can help you develop longer articles for magazines and regional papers that will attract a larger audience to your open houses.

• Develop a cross marketing program

Cross marketing uses a variety of media to reinforce your message and generate traffic through your homes. Medallion Homes in San Antonio uses a variety of marketing channels to reinforce one another. Carrie Gehlbach, VP Sales and Marketing, describes their approach. "Our newspaper ads and morning radio spots send them to the web site. From the web site they can order a CD-ROM and that sends them to the model home. Our focus is to get them to the model homes. We've sold about 60 homes from our web site alone."

By using interactive media like the CD-ROM and the web site they are able to provide prospective buyers with a greater amount of information and pictures before they arrive on site. By doing so, the sales staff has more time to qualify the buyer and close the sale while the customer is in the sales office.

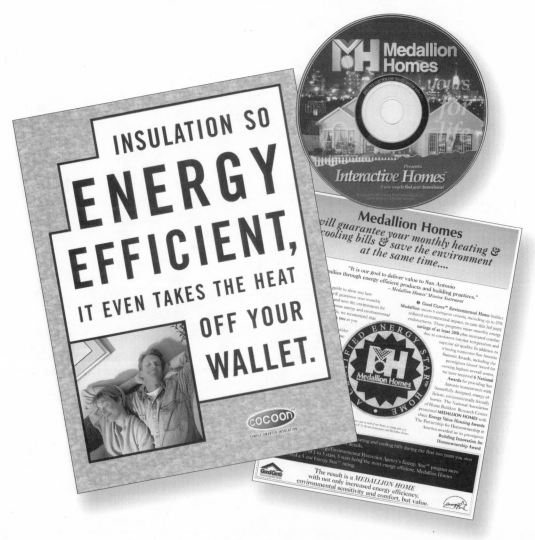

• **Put your signature on your projects.**

Bill Eich leaves a mark on his Iowa homes. He says, "One of the most effective things we do to market ourselves is to affix a brass kick plate on the home with the year it was built and our logo. Our ads show me putting the kick plate on after final inspection. It is a symbol of our signature on the home, and it makes our clients' homes something special."

Emphasize the Benefits to the Buyers

Marc Richmond-Powers suggests that builders keep this in mind: "What the homebuyer is getting out of a green building is a higher quality building that is going to be healthier for them. And in doing so, homebuyers are going to be able to do their part to help preserve the environment. I believe that is something that everyone wants to do, but people don't know how to. This is a way that they can do it, feel good about it, and feel good about their own home as well as for the future of their children. It is very empowering. You are giving people an opportunity to make that contribution to the world through the biggest purchase of their life. The home buying process is overwhelming for people, especially first time homebuyers for whom the whole situation is an anxiety-ridden experience. There are so many questions to ask and so many options and choices to make and so much money riding on it, and everyone is stretching to the limit. It is an overwhelming process. When you offer buyers a green home which is secure and solid and has meaning to it, that brings a lot more happiness to the whole process."

As a management consultant to the building industry, Al Trellis' advice in the Home Builder's Network brochure *Managing Your Custom Building Business for Profit* can be applied to marketing green homes.

A green version of 20 ways to sell a home by Al Trellis:

1. *Create your image in association with green building*
2. *Be consistent*
3. *Win an award*
4. *Get involved*
5. *Speak to local groups*
6. *Teach a course*
7. *Solicit testimonials*
8. *Give a party*
9. *Ask for referrals*
10. *Reward referrals*
11. *Don't be shy or modest*
12. *Offer "free" services*
13. *Build a reputation as an expert*
14. *Show your expertise*
15. *Get your name in the paper*
16. *Hire a photographer*
17. *Keep a photo album in the office*
18. *Mount photos on the wall*
19. *Have a good brochure*
20. *Believe you're the best*

- Develop a comprehensive green marketing plan.
- Promote your homes in a way that emphasizes the "green difference."
- Develop clever and unusual outlets for your message.
- Train your sales force and realtors to focus on the difference.
- Use your satisfied clients as a powerful referral base.

"Marketing green in a black and white world" requires standing out in the highly competitive world of marketing new homes. When you are building green you have a new story to tell that homebuyers want to hear. But to get your message to them you have to be creative and rise above all of the advertising chatter that bombards consumers everyday. By creating innovative events, by working closely with the media, and by finding co-marketing partners that share your buyer's demographics, you can make your homes as unique in the eyes of the public as they are different from the competition's homes.

The Sales Approach

6

Learning to sell green homes means learning the language necessary to communicate the benefits of green features to your buyers. The beginning of this chapter focuses on how to connect with your buyer. The second part, provides explanations of the benefits of individual green features.

Keys to Sales - Important elements of the sales approach include understanding how your product addresses customers' environmental concerns and connecting with your buyers' self-interest.

Connecting Green Building Features with Sales - Features from the Denver Built Green Checklist, complimented with an explanation of their benefits, provides sales language to help you sell your homes. Your sales people can tell buyers how specific energy efficiency, resource conservation, and indoor air quality features benefit them.

Sales Approach to Green Features and Benefits - Environmental features arranged by benefits to help you develop a comprehensive sales approach.

Keys to Sales

—— Connecting With Buyers' Values ——

As we said in the beginning of this book, green building is more about people than it is about technology. Selling homes is where it all comes together because this is where green technology most clearly connects with people. Sales people can communicate to buyers the benefits of buying green for health, quality of life, and their children's well being.

A house is just a building. A home is where people's lives happen. Selling green is a "heart sell." Realtors have told me they can sell conventional real estate all day long and never connect with a deeper part of themselves, but it comes out when they sell green homes. It doesn't matter who the buyers are or what their status in the world might be. When it comes to their children, they are all moms and dads. They make decisions that go deeper than just addressing potential resale value.

Good real estate sales people learn how to "read" what is important to the family as they walk through a home. Facial expressions, body language, time spent in each room, and questions to the sales people convey something about the buyers' values. *Selling Green in a Black and White World* can bring values right up front. For example, when questions about schools come up, realtors can discuss the healthy indoor air quality of a green home, since formaldehyde and other chemicals used in conventional home construction can impact a child's ability to learn in school.

A family's concerns about the future can also influence their decision to buy a home. When buyers are shown green features, they can see the home as an investment in the collective future. Buying green is a step that lets homebuyers contribute to the greater whole and support the best interest of not only their child, but the world's children.

——— Merchandising and Sales ———

Sales people need good merchandising support. A sales office can be a place that features examples of products and stories about green building technology. For example, McStain created the "Green Building Museum," a place where prospective buyers could touch and feel green and environmental products that are typically hidden in the walls. The sales staff used the museum to discuss the benefits of products used in McStain homes.

——— Communicating With ———
Potential Buyers

To communicate about environmental features and benefits with buyers, the sales staff needs to:

- Be aware of the most common areas of concern: energy efficiency, indoor air quality, and resource conservation.

- Understand the environmental features in the homes as they relate to and help alleviate those concerns.

- Communicate how the home-buyer will benefit from the purchase of the green home.

Remember that environmentally conscious buyers want to hear the whole story. When sales people understand the big picture, they can talk comfortably about environmental features and tell convincing stories about their benefits.

Ron Jones says that many buyers are already predisposed to reduce the environmental impact of their lifestyles. If information is readily available to them, people are more inclined to make the choice for

Ron Jones, Owner
Sierra Custom Builders
Placitas, New Mexico
(505) 867-0157
Ron Jones is president of the New Mexico HBA, the chairman of the National Green Builder Subcommittee, and serves on the NAHB board of directors. His company, Sierra Custom Builders, works in custom homes, spec homes, and developments in the Santa Fe and Albuquerque markets. They build one to three homes per year. In 1995, Jones received Custom Builder Magazine*'s Custom Home of the Year Award—Best in the Southwest Region, for an original design project in Santa Fe. Even before the New Mexico green building program was in place, Ron Jones was already doing everything on the checklist.*

green features.

—— Selling the Sizzle: ——
The Non-Monetary Benefits of Buying Green

Environmental   features

Immediate Move-In Available

Medallion homeowner Stephen Lancaster entertains his neighbors each month when he celebrates opening his low utility bills!

"I love opening my utility bill!"
- Medallion Homeowner Stephen Lancaster

"My Medallion Home *saves me money each month on utility and water bills, and my home's outstanding energy features ensure maximum comfort on sweltering summer afternoons."*

FAMILY ROOM
MASTER SUITE
CASUAL DINING AREA
PANTRY
KITCHEN
BEDROOM 2

"Don't sign anything until you've visited a Medallion Home. Just look how happy Medallion's made me!"

that address health are not as easy to price tag as energy efficient features that save the consumer dollars each month. They are, however, just as important and are often more relevant to an individual's well being. One such issue is indoor air quality. Saving old-growth forests may be a greater stretch, yet it can be just the issue that gets some people's attention.

John Friesenhahn, C.O.O.
Medallion Homes, San Antonio, Texas
(210) 494-2555
Medallion Homes grew out of a development company in 1995. They build primarily entry-level and first move-up homes starting at $80,000, with an average price in the $130,000s. Building 360 homes this year, Medallion is a three-time winner of the Energy Value Housing Award and was named EVHA Builder of the Year 2000. They also won two 1999 Best in American Living Awards for building the Best Affordable Home in the Nation. In addition, Medallion is certified a Good Cents™ Environmental Homebuilder, as an Energy Star™ Builder, and they guarantee their homes' annual heating and cooling costs through the Engineered for Life™ Program. Medallion Homes is a leader in marketing techniques for green homes and in training their sales staff.

A good example of explaining non-monetary benefits happened when I was hired to conduct a one day training program for local managers of a southern utility company. The utility was introducing a green building program and wanted all the local managers to understand the program and why it was important to their customers. In an era of utility deregulation, the company felt it would be a way to create greater customer loyalty.

I started the program talking about the environmental problems the planet was facing. I went through global warming, population growth, ozone depletion, and the need for buildings to be built more resourcefully. It was like talking to a blank wall. These managers lived in the deep South and were in the business of selling electricity, not saving the planet. I knew I had about a minute and a half to capture their attention and rescue the rest of the day.

When I started talking about old growth forests I had an idea. I asked the audience how many of them hunted and fished. There was a pause while they refocused their attention on me and away from the one window across the room. I asked again, and all of their hands went up. I asked whether they had experienced any difference in the number of birds and wildlife in the last decade or so.

Hands flew up. "You bet!" said one. Another chimed in, "It used to be that you could go out into the country and point your rifle into the woods and hit a deer, there were so many of them. It's a tree farm now. You never see deer in them woods." Hunting and fishing stories were going around the room. These guys were in familiar territory now and fully present. When the energy died down a bit I cut back in and said, "That's exactly why it is so important to look for alternatives to solid sawn lumber. Once the forest ecosystem is destroyed, the wildlife don't come back for many years." "Yes sir, buddy!" said the local manager. "I can get behind that." They were with me for the rest of the day. They actually told me at the end that this was one of the better workshops that the utility company had provided for them.

→ The moral of the story is you have to speak to people "where they live." People only care about the big picture if it comes back to their own self-interest.

Connecting Green Building Features with Sales

The following checklist contains representative features from the Denver HBA Built Green Program. The list will help your sales people explain green benefits to buyers. The checklist is broken down by building category. (See the full checklist in Appendix A.)

Each section begins with environmental concerns pertinent to that category and ends with benefits to the buyer for each feature listed. Your sales people can use the language in the "benefits" sections to communicate effectively with your buyers. For example, if you are including low-E windows in your homes, your sales staff can turn to that category and find just the right words to explain the benefits to the buyer.

Land Use: Lot

Environmental Concerns

Typical new construction creates tons of debris. Home construction can produce up to five tons of waste per house. Job site wastes include metals, wood and cardboard, which represent over 50 percent of the debris normally taken to landfills.

Topsoil is one of our most rapidly vanishing resources. It is our richest, most valuable, yet thinnest layer of soil. Scraped off during construction, it is costly to replace later for landscaping.

Outdoor structures like decks often use wood preserved with toxic chemicals. These can be easily avoided.

Benefits of Features

• Trees and natural features on site have been protected during construction.

Benefit: Mature trees help shade the home in summer, keeping it cooler and more comfortable. Trees on the north and west sides provide a windscreen in the winter, keeping the house warmer. Mature trees also increase the value of the property.

• Topsoil will be saved and reused.

Benefit: Saving topsoil saves money by not having to bring in as much new soil for landscaping and lawns. Topsoil is the most valuable soil for landscaping and gardening your yard.

• **Home placement saves east and south lot areas for outdoor use.**

Benefit: Southern outdoor areas are warmer in winter so they can be used for more months of the year.

• **Outdoor structures, decking, and landscaping materials are made from recycled materials or pressure-treated engineered lumber.**

Benefit: Recycled-content outdoor materials can be more durable than treated solid lumber. Some will last for decades without painting or staining. Pressure-treated engineered lumber also saves large old growth trees.

• **Home is oriented on lot such that the long dimension faces within 30 degrees of south.**

Benefit: Orientation to the south increases passive solar gain and potential for solar retrofit.

Waste Management

Environmental Concerns

Americans today generate over four pounds of household waste per person per day. Only 17 percent of that is recycled. Waste generated goes to increasingly crowded landfills and some waste virtually never breaks down.

Benefits of Features

• **Provide a built-in kitchen recycling center to include two bins.**

Benefit: Today Americans recycle seven times more waste than 10 years ago. Built-in bins make it possible to manage recycling efforts.

• **Job site waste is minimized by using materials wisely and by prohibiting burying construction debris.**

Benefit: Using materials effectively increases the value of the home by reducing waste.

• **Job site waste is recycled.**

Benefit: Up to 60 percent of job site waste can be easily recycled. Recycling diverts trash from the waste stream that can be converted into new, usable materials and building products.

——— Energy Use: Envelope ———

Environmental Concerns

The envelope of the house is the greatest source of heat transmission, causing uncomfortable indoor temperatures. Air infiltration is a major culprit of heat loss. Inefficient windows are the other major part of the home's envelope which contributes to temperature swings, resulting in higher energy use to keep the house comfortable all year round.

Benefits of Features

• **South glass area is between 5 to 7 percent of total finished floor area.**

Benefit: By sun tempering the home, the south facing windows reduce heating requirements by 10-20 percent, lowering utility bills.

• **Advanced sealing has been performed on the house.**

Benefit: Foaming and caulking the areas of potential infiltration reduces drafts and makes the home more comfortable in winter.

• **Blower door testing has shown that the air infiltration rate of the home is less than .35 air changes per hour.**

Benefit: Houses breathe by exchanging outdoor air with indoor air through cracks and penetrations in the envelope. The less air exchange there is, the more energy efficient the home. The blower door test determines how much heat the house loses through infiltration. Below .35 ACH requires make up air or ventilation to provide fresh air to occupants.

• **Energy heels of 6" or more on trusses.**

Benefit: Energy heels provide for insulation to be installed above the wall to reduce heat loss and improve comfort.

——— Energy Use: Mechanical Systems ———

Environmental Concerns

In new construction, mechanical systems are often an afterthought. Design and installation of mechanical systems often leads to unwanted heat loss through poorly or unsealed ductwork. Too many mechanical systems are oversized, so they cycle frequently which lowers unit efficiency thereby increasing utility costs.

Benefits of Features

• **Furnace is centrally located and all duct runs are reduced as much as possible.**

Benefit: When the furnace is far away from where you want heat, especially in the master suite, the air is cooled by the time it reaches the room and comfort is compromised. A centrally located furnace leads to greater comfort in the winter.

• **Thermostat features an on switch for furnace fan to circulate air.**

Benefit: During most of the spring, summer, and fall just moving air can keep a house comfortable. The fan switch allows you to circulate air on the warmest days making the house more comfortable without the expense of air conditioning.

• **Sealed combustion gas fireplace or sealed wood-burning fireplace or stove with outside combustion air.**

Benefit: Sealed combustion means that the air needed for the flame comes from the outside directly. Otherwise, occupants would be competing for oxygen with the burning process. Sealing the fireplace is necessary to keep heat in. If unsealed, the fireplace requires two to three times more energy than it provides to the home simply by exhausting heat from the house up the chimney. Gas fireplaces also reduce outdoor air pollution.

• **Set back programmable thermostat.**

Benefit: People want the house warmer when they are lounging in the evening or on weekends than at night when they sleep. By letting the electronics remember for you, it automatically saves energy during the hours when no one is home or everyone is asleep.

• **Furnace ductwork joints sealed with low toxic mastic.**

Benefit: Ducts lose air at each joint like a hole in a bucket. Duct tape dries out in a few years and loses its sealing ability. Mastic stays flexible for much longer, assuring that heat gets where it is supposed to go. Sealed ducts are also safer, reducing the potential for combustion gasses (carbon monoxide) to enter the living space.

• **Whole house fan installed.**

Benefit: A whole house fan is much more energy efficient than air conditioning. Comfort is maintained by drawing outside air in during all but the hottest days.

—— Energy Use: Indoor Air Quality ——

Environmental Concerns

Indoor air quality can be compromised in several ways: by carbon monoxide escaping from furnaces and hot water heaters; by car exhaust containing toxic chemicals entering the house from attached garages; by off-gassing from building materials, furniture, and fabrics; by unburned hydrocarbons resulting from cooking; and by the stir of dust inside the house.

Benefits of Features

- **Sealed-combustion furnace**
- **Sealed-combustion hot water heater.**

Benefit: Carbon monoxide, a by-product of combustion, is a potential source of indoor air problems. By isolating the combustion gases, they will never migrate into the living space. Sealed units also eliminate the need for cold make-up air ducts in the basement that create drafts in adjacent areas.

- **Exhaust fan in garage on timer or wired to door opener.**

Benefit: Exhausting car exhaust can be one of the most cost-effective measures for improving indoor air quality.

- **Heat recovery ventilator (HRV) or air-to-air heat exchanger installed.**

Benefit: An HRV dramatically improves indoor air quality by diluting indoor with fresh air. It recaptures heat from the exhaust stream, which saves money on utility bills.

- **Radon vent pipe for retrofit has been installed.**

Benefit: Radon is a suspected human carcinogen. It comes from the soil or from concrete. Care has been taken to ensure that if radon is ever discovered in the home, it will be easy to install fans to evacuate it from the living space.

- **All range hoods are vented to the outside.**

Benefit: Unburned hydrocarbons can result from cooking. More than smells, these particles are not healthy to breathe. Range hoods that vent directly outside eliminate exposure to hydrocarbons, overheating, and excess moisture build-up in the kitchen.

Energy Use: Water Heating

Environmental Concerns

Water heating impacts both water consumption and energy use. Heat is lost from hot water pipes as the water travels from the tank to the shower or sink. If it is a long distance, water is wasted as you wait for the water to warm up at the faucet or shower-head. Inefficient hot water heaters use fuel that could be offset by solar energy.

Benefits of Features

• **Gas water heater has an energy factor of more than .60.**

Benefit: New hot water heater technology provides improved energy efficient hot water heaters for a small additional cost. Efficient heaters save money every month as long as the home is owned.

• **Hot water pipes are insulated to R=6 in unconditioned spaces.**

Benefit: By keeping water hot 24 hours a day, some heat is lost all the time. Insulating the pipes reduces the heat loss and helps provide hot water faster in distant sinks and showers.

• **Gas water heater with insulating blanket installed to manufacturer's specifications.**

Benefit: An insulating blanket is an inexpensive way to reduce heat loss from hot water stored in the tank.

• **Rough-in for future solar hot water heating.**

Benefit: For houses oriented such that solar collectors can be retrofitted, this is a great sales feature for saving customers installation costs in the future when solar is more prominent.

Energy Use: Appliances

Environmental Concerns

Appliances use electricity and water with varying degrees of efficiency. Some refrigerators today use twice as much energy as older models. Electric heating and cooking is inefficient compared to gas. Every kilowatt hour (kwh) used adds over two pounds of CO^2 to the atmosphere.

Benefits of Features

- **Dishwasher with energy-saving cycle.**

Benefit: In many climates dishes can air dry in the washer and save energy used by the electric resistance heater inside.

- **Refrigerator less than $66 estimated annual electric cost.**

Benefit: Energy efficient refrigerators are available that use 2/3 or less electricity than conventional models.

- **If appliances are not included, a list of energy efficient appliances is provided.**

Benefit: Energy efficient appliances can save from $50 - $200 per year in electricity bills. Energy saving features in dishwashers save not only electricity, but water as well.

- **Solar electric system provides 20 percent or more of the home's electricity.**

Benefit: Grid-tied photovoltaic systems are becoming increasingly popular for emergency lighting backup and for energy self-reliance. In states with a buy-back program, the system can spin the electric meter backward–saving on electricity bills.

——— Energy Use: Lighting ———

Environmental Concerns

Incandescent light bulbs are an inefficient means of generating light. Natural daylighting is more attractive to buyers. Dark houses that do not receive much natural light through windows cost more to light and are less pleasant for the inhabitants.

Benefits of Features

- **Light colored walls, ceiling, and carpet.**

Benefit: Natural light makes people happier and healthier. With good placement of windows and by keeping surfaces light colored, the need for daytime electric lighting is reduced.

- **Furnish four compact fluorescent light bulbs to owners.**

Benefit: Compact fluorescent bulbs are four times more efficient than conventional bulbs and last 10 times longer. One bulb can save enough energy in its lifetime to drive a compact car coast to coast.

- **No recessed-lighting fixtures installed in insulated ceilings or insulated fixtures have been used.**

Benefit: Because of the heat build-up inside the typical recessed light fixtures, the insulation in ceilings must be spaced away from light fixtures. The result of that space is like keeping a window open all winter long. Special insulated fixtures prevent the drafty effect of the older recessed fixture design.

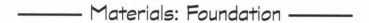

——— Materials: Foundation ———

Environmental Concerns

Forming concrete foundations can account for 15-35 percent of the total cost of concrete installations. Essentially, the foundation gets built twice, once in wood and again in concrete. Rigid foam forming systems stay in place and provide permanent insulation for the basement. Some companies have invested in aluminum forms that can be reused. This becomes a more resource-efficient solution, although it adds labor in building and dismantling forms.

Benefits of Features

• **Western coal fly ash concrete has been used in foundation.**

Benefit: Fly ash is a by-product of coal-fired power plants. By mixing it with concrete, not only is the foundation stronger, but it also diverts the fly ash from landfills.

• **Insulated foundation with Rigid R=8 foam insulation.**

Benefit: Several alternatives use Styrofoam in a variety of shapes and sizes to form walls. The foam forms stay in place and serve as high efficiency insulation for the foundation. This saves energy and increases comfort. By installing rigid foam outside the foundation wall it is unnecessary to have batts or spray-insulated walls in the basement when finishing the space.

• **Frost-protected shallow foundation.**

Benefit: Shallow foundations are a resource efficient way to save money on construction costs without compromising the structural integrity of the home.

——— Materials: Structural Frame ———

Environmental Concerns

Large dimension lumber (2x10 and larger) is often milled from old-growth trees, which depletes our ancient forests and uses only 65 percent of the cellulose fiber from the trees. Many new homes use up to 300 old-growth trees and require an acre of forest to be harvested for construction.

Benefits of Features

- **Engineered wood I-joists used for floors.**
- **Trusses or I-joists are used for roofs.**
- **Engineered lumber products for beams, joists, or headers.**

Benefits: Engineered wood, especially I-joists are now cost-competitive for most applications, use fast-growing farm trees for cellulose fiber, and can use up to 90 percent of the potential fiber. Engineered lumber products often use fast- growing farm trees that require 50 percent less wood fiber to perform the same structural functions better. Using I-joists results in a stronger home with straighter walls, floors, and ceilings.

- **The house has been built with optimum value engineering framing.**

Benefit: This technique was developed to get the maximum strength from the frame while accommodating insulation in places that have conventionally been sources of heat loss, such as corners and wall intersections. It also saves money in framing costs.

———— Materials: Roof ————

Environmental Concerns

Petrochemical products are still the base for most residential roofing products. These conventional products only have a 15 or 25-year life span, which makes them resource-intensive, since shingles are rarely recycled. Once old shingles are taken to a landfill, these materials virtually never break down. Toxins from shingles leach into landfill soil and then into the groundwater.

Benefits of Features

- **Minimum 30-year concrete roofing installed.**

Benefit: Typical asphalt roofing must be replaced after 15 years. Alternatives are available in steel, plastic, and cement that use recycled content materials and come in shake or shingle styles. All have longer life spans than asphalt or fiberglass shingles and can be recycled. Concrete roofing saves money over the life of the home and is fireproof.

- **Class A—Fiberglass roofing has been installed.**

Benefit: Fiberglass composition shingles are fire and hail resistant, available in many styles and colors, and keep the house affordable. Forty-year life saves replacement costs over shorter life shingles.

Materials: Exterior Walls

Environmental Concerns

Wood siding contributes to the over-harvesting of our forests because to be effective, it requires either clear material free of knots, or large, ancient cedar or redwood trees to be harvested. Pine siding is a poor alternative because it can warp, split, or crack and needs to be repainted frequently.

Benefits of Features

• **Oriented Strand Board (OSB) used for sheathing.**

Benefit: OSB is made from fast-growing farm trees and unlike conventional plywood, it does not require old growth trees to be cut.

• **Recycled or reconstituted content siding.**
• **Reconstituted or recycled-content fascia, soffit or trim.**

Benefit: Siding that has been engineered from wood fiber will not crack, split, or warp and holds paint longer, reducing maintenance costs.

• **Natural or synthetic stucco used.**

Benefit: Stucco increases insulation, reduces air infiltration and drafts inside the home, and reduces maintenance costs compared to wood siding.

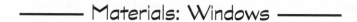

Materials: Windows

Environmental Concerns

Windows lose heat through the frame and through the glass. They also let in cold air between the window and the framing material surrounding it. Good windows make the whole house more comfortable. Low-E glass coating, which increases glass R-value to 3 is increasing in market share each year. The premium of 10-15 percent for low-E easily pays for itself in a few years. The added benefit is that the window is warmer and therefore more comfortable to be near in cold weather.

Benefits of Features

• **Windows are double-glazed with 1/2" air space.**

Benefit: A minimum air space of 1/2" reduces heat loss through the glass.

- **Wood frames.**

Benefit: Over the last 15 years, the effective R-value of windows has increased by 50 percent. This is the result of both improvements in glazing and in frame construction.

- **Vinyl frames.**

Benefit: Vinyl frame windows are energy efficient, very durable, and never need painting.

- **Low-E windows.**

Benefit: Low-E is a coating that reflects heat in on cold nights and out on summer days. It not only increases the R-value of the window by 50 percent, it makes indoor space much more comfortable year round.

——— Materials: Sub-Floor ———

Environmental Concerns

Plywood requires large diameter trees to effectively peel the plies for lamination. Most OSB (and plywood) uses phenol-formaldehyde adhesive that is less toxic than urea-formaldehyde but still off-gasses formaldehyde into the house. Some OSB uses an even less toxic MDI resin base for its adhesive.

Benefits of Features

- **Oriented Strand Board (OSB) used for sub-floors.**

Benefit: OSB is another engineered wood product that reduces the demand for old-growth trees while improving the quality of the sub-floor. OSB uses a variety of sources for cellulose fiber and adhesive types. OSB can be manufactured from fast-growing "weed" trees and uses a higher percentage of the tree. OSB in conjunction with wood I-joist floor framing can reduce cellulose fiber requirements by 50 percent with superior structural integrity.

——— Materials: Doors ———

Environmental Concerns

Luan is a tropical hardwood that has been used for decades in new U.S. home construction. Excessive harvesting of Luan has left areas of the Asian-Pacific devastated. Exterior doors are basically solid wood or foam wrapped in metal or some other weather-resistant material. Most insulated doors are relatively similar in energy efficiency since the market is so competitive. The key components in an efficient door are good weather-stripping and an effective threshold. R-values of 5-7 are common.

Benefits of Features

• **No Luan interior doors used.**

Benefit: A decrease in Luan harvesting means less devastation to Pacific Rim forests.

• **Reconstituted or recycled content hardboard doors have been used.**

OR

• **Solid domestically grown interior wood pane doors have been used.**

Benefit: Reconstituted hardboard uses wood waste to create a paintable and durable door that is stronger than Luan and does not harm the forests. Doors made from domestically grown farm wood can also be used instead of Luan.

Materials: Finish Floor

Environmental Concerns

Vinyl tile and other sheet flooring products whose primary component is polyvinyl chloride (PVC) create VOC off-gassing. Toxic by-products are generally produced in their manufacture. The EPA has identified carpet as a potential source of indoor air pollution. Carpet harbors dust, lead, pesticides, and other harmful chemicals, including formaldehyde, which is used to glue carpet in place.

Benefits of Features

• **Recycled content carpet pad.**

Benefit: Recycled carpet pad is constituted of waste from the carpet industry, providing the same comfort of a conventional carpet pad.

• **Recycled content carpet.**

Benefit: Creating a use for pop bottles diverts them from the landfill. Carpet made from recycled pop bottles is competitively priced and is more naturally stain-resistant than virgin fibers used in conventional carpet.

- **Ceramic tile installed with low toxic mastic and grout.**

Benefit: Ceramic tile is durable and long lasting. Non-toxic mastic and grout have been selected to minimize the number of toxic chemicals introduced into the house.

— Materials: Finishes And Adhesives —

Environmental Concerns

More than any other category, these products adversely affect indoor air quality, especially immediately after installation. The health hazard is particularly acute for installers. Most conventional products off-gas VOCs, formaldehyde, and other chemicals that are generally used to enhance the performance and shelf-life of the product. VOCs are what produce that "new house" smell. VOCs are not healthy to breathe, however. In addition, floor finishes can be one of the most toxic elements in the home. The chemicals found in these finishes off-gas for months creating an unhealthy indoor environment. The toxicity of combined chemicals on human health is a major medical concern. Quality substitutions that are lower in toxicity or are non-toxic are now available for all of these products.

Benefits of Features

- **Paints and finishes contain minimal volatile organic compounds (VOCs).**

Benefit: Lower VOC paints improve indoor air quality by reducing exposure to VOCs.

- **Water-based urethane finishes used on wood floors.**

Benefit: Water-based finishes are much less toxic than conventional solvent based products and are durable and attractive.

—— Materials: Cabinetry And Trim ——

Environmental Concerns

Particleboard is one of the largest sources of formaldehyde, a suspected human carcinogen. It can off-gas for five years into the living environment. It is typically used for cabinet boxes, substrates in counter tops, shelving, and stair treads. Alternatives to particleboard are available that are formaldehyde-free. Any use of particleboard should be sealed with a low permeability coating.

Benefits of Features

• **Any exposed particleboard is painted with water-based sealer inside cabinets, underside of countertops.**

Benefit: Painting edges reduces the off-gassing of formaldehyde into the living space of the home and is an inexpensive partial solution to the problem.

• **No tropical hardwoods have been used unless from certified sustainably-managed forests.**

Benefit: Tropical hardwoods are the lungs of the planet, keeping our atmosphere healthy. Sustainably managed forests reduce the number of hardwoods cut.

• **Finger-jointed trim.**

Benefit: Clear wood trim gets more expensive as we deplete our ancient forests. Finger-jointed trim is resource efficient by using short pieces of clear wood glued together to create painted finished doors and windows that are straighter and more stable than conventional clear wood.

——— Water Conservation ———

Environmental Concerns

Conserving water saves energy and reduces our need for water and waste treatment. By installing water-efficient faucets and showerheads, a typical family can save $60-120 per year. That translates into roughly 17,000 gallons of water saved. Typical showerheads use 3.5-6 gal/min. A water-efficient showerhead reduces the flow to less than 2.5 gal/min. without sacrificing water pressure.

Benefits of Features

• **Grass has been planted that uses less water in lawn areas.**

Benefit: Buffalo grass and tall-type fescues can reduce watering requirements by half.

• **Xeriscaping with native, drought-resistant plants.**
• **A list of other native, drought-resistant plants has been provided.**

Benefit: Xeriscaping with drought resistant plants can be more beautiful than plain lawn and reduce outside watering dramatically.

Sales Approach to Green Features and Benefits

Immediate Benefits of Green Features

Benefits to homeowners of environmental features
- *Lower initial cost of products*
- *Lower monthly costs*
- *Improved resale*
- *More comfortable*
- *Quieter*
- *Improved indoor air quality*
- *Greater safety*
- *Higher quality materials*
- *More durable*
- *Less maintenance*

Most of the features listed above help create overall environmental benefits. Other more immediate benefits can accrue to the homeowner.

When initiating a green marketing strategy, base it on what your buyers want most. Different buyer types are swayed by different sets of benefits. In most cases, the top of the list is lower costs. With today's busy lifestyles, lower maintenance and higher durability can mean fewer weekends devoted to "honey do's."

Features Grouped by Benefit

By clustering green features around specific benefits, it is easier to establish the marketing strategy for a project. The following is a list of features broken down by the collective benefits they produce:

Lower Costs

Site and Land Use
- House or addition oriented for passive solar heating.

Foundation
- Permanent R=9 rigid exterior insulation.
- R-4.5 Insulation under entire heated slab.
- Wall and Roof Insulation
- Increase wall insulation to R-24.
- Increase ceiling insulation to R-38.
- Cellulose insulation sprayed into wall cavities.
- HCFC-free rigid foam sprayed into wall cavities.

Windows and Doors
- Wood frames.
- Low-E glass.
- Heat mirror windows.
- Exterior R-5 doors.

Cabinetry and Trim

- Finger-jointed wood trim.
- Hardwood veneer trim.
- Recycled cabinets or trim materials.

Water

- Low water grasses planted.
- Xeriscape > 40% of yard.
- 1.5 GPM bath faucets.
- Front-loading clothes washer.
- Low water dishwasher.
- On-demand hot water switch.

 ## Greater Comfort

Site/Land Use

- Home or addition located with south exposure.

Foundation

- Permanent R=9 rigid insulation.
- R-4.5 insulation under entire heated slab.

Indoor Air Quality

- Crawl space vapor barrier installed.
- Crawl space vapor barrier sealed.

Water

- On-demand hot water switch.

 ## Improved Indoor Air Quality

Sub-Floor

- Urea formaldehyde-free material.

Insulation

- Cellulose insulation used throughout home.
- Formaldehyde-free insulation used.
- Non-toxic spray foam insulation used.

Cabinetry and Trim

- No particleboard used inside house.
- Particleboard cabinets, shelves, counter tops sealed with no-VOC sealer.
- Low toxic cabinet finishes.
- Formaldehyde-free cabinets.
- Recycled cabinets or trim materials.

Finish Floor
- Ceramic tile with low toxic adhesives.
- Water-based floor finishes.
- Non-toxic sealer on masonry floors.

Finishes and Adhesives
- Low or no-VOC paints.
- Recycled-content paint.
- Solvent-free adhesives.
- Water-based wood finishes.

Indoor Air Quality Measures
- Sealed combustion furnace or boiler.
- Sealed combustion hot water heater.
- Exhaust fan in attached garage.
- Heat recovery ventilator.
- Radon mitigation installed.
- Mechanical room enclosed R=11.
- Ductwork sealed with mastic.
- Range hood vented to outside.
- HEPA filter installed.
- Carbon monoxide detector.
- Crawl space vapor barrier installed.
- Craw space vapor barrier sealed.

 ## More Durable / Less Maintenance

Exterior Walls
- Local brick.
- Indigenous stone.
- Stucco.
- Cement siding.

Roof
- 30 - 50 year roofing.
- Fiber-cement roofing.

Finish Floor
- Recycled content carpet.
- Natural fiber carpet.
- Natural linoleum.

Finishes and Adhesives
- Ductwork sealed with mastic.

Conclusion

Sales is everything. It doesn't matter how well the house is built, how green it is, or what a good company you have created if your sales staff doesn't communicate value to your customers. Typically realtors are most comfortable talking about kitchens and master suites, the features of a home they think the customer is most interested in. It takes time to get them as comfortable with green features and benefits as they are with traditional sales approaches. Taking the time to train the sales staff is one of the best investments you can make in your entire company.

"We train all of our new sales people for two weeks before they go into the field," says Vernon McKown. "We teach them our philosophy of sales and how to help our customers make informed decisions. We have a thick sales manual with scripts and details. There are many elements to building, and it's hard for the sales staff to focus on all of them, so we give them a toolbox full of tools to sell a house. The bottom line is we add value by what we do."

McKown also conducts weekly sales training meetings that include role-playing. Sales staff are placed in new situations that develop their selling abilities. "Mystery shoppers" are sent out to the field see how well sales staff do.

"Today's consumers are the best educated ever. They respond well to information. That's where a lot of builders miss out. They aren't incorporating green into their sales," says McKown.

Sales staff buy-in and training are critical to your success in "selling green in a black and white world." No matter what products you use, no matter what your vision is, if you can't translate the benefits of what you are doing to your sales staff and have them understand it, accept it, and rally around it, your chances of success are slim.

To assure the success of your green building effort, the sales staff needs to fully understand that you are adding value to their customers and to their sales process. They ultimately have the most to gain from the new green homes you are building. When they are your greatest advocates, when they feel truly empowered by the changes and are confident in the benefits, they will have the tools to close the sale that might have gotten away.

Case Studies 7

The case studies in this chapter can give you valuable insight on individual companies and the lessons they learned as they went through the process of **Building Green in a Black and White World.** You will learn what worked, what didn't, and why.

McStain Enterprises, Colorado - Green goes mainstream. A production builder begins with an environmental research house and now incorporates green into all their homes.

Behind the Walls Expo, Florida - Inviting his customers to peek behind the walls sells Philip Russell's custom homes.

Dewees Island, South Carolina - Designed with the belief that man and nature can co-exist healthfully, this private island development takes green beyond the walls.

McStain Enterprises Colorado

——— The Art of Building ——— with the Long View

Most developers in the black and white world build with short term objectives in mind. The number of units per acre, lead time for permits, availability of trades, and short sales cycles drive planning decisions. Maintaining the bottom line for quarterly financial reports is fundamental for them in doing good business.

McStain is as concerned as any one about doing good business. The difference is their perspective. "I once flew over a European city and saw the land planning of 1000 years ago. I realized the decisions we make in each new development will affect people for a long time. The streets and buildings we create will impact the environment from now on," says Tom Hoyt.

The responsibility Hoyt is talking about goes beyond land use and siting issues. Building construction uses over 40 percent of this country's natural resources, particularly wood products. Buildings consume 35 percent of the energy used each year. "Our responsibility goes deeper than the project," says Hoyt. "We have a responsibility to be as environmentally sensitive as possible. We have to consider how sustainable our practices are, the impact on the environment, and the health of our buyers. We have to help our customers make better long-term decisions."

This thinking was the genesis of the Environmental Research House. McStain wanted to know how the materials and methods of green home building affect the larger environment and the indoor environment. "People in Boulder County care about the environment. They want to live lifestyles that support environmental integrity. This house was our attempt to discover what works and what doesn't in environmental building options so we could assure our customers that their homes make sense and are affordable," explains Hoyt.

McStain's product selection process took into account several factors. New products had to:

1. Reduce environmental impact. That included using recycled content in manufacturing, fewer resources to perform the same function, durable products to reduce replacement costs, and less valuable and costly components.

2. Compare favorably in structure or aesthetics with conventional products.

3. Be cost-effective. The products could not be so expensive that they were out of the buyer's reach.

4. Fit the existing construction process: that is, not be so unique that trades contractors couldn't use them. That included local availability, purchasing through existing suppliers, and easy installation.

5. Not to be a warranty issue for either the buyer or for McStain.

Hundreds of products were reviewed. About 30 were selected for substitution.

—— Environmental Research House ——

The primary intention of the research house was to discover solutions that could easily be incorporated into their production building operation. In 1994, project manager George Russell began researching a list of possible substitute materials, systems, manufacturers, and suppliers appropriate for McStain's three areas of interest:

- maximizing energy efficiency
- minimizing long-term health risks by improving indoor air quality
- using resource efficient and environmentally responsible building materials

A model currently in production was selected for modification to incorporate the new systems and products. The criteria for the project were stringent. The design had to look like the other houses in their portfolio. It had to have the same curb appeal that made their houses so popular. Products had to be available in the Colorado market and they had to be of high quality.

The outcome was a home that was visually indistinguishable from neighboring houses, yet it functioned in a radically different manner.

Energy Efficiency

An energy-efficient package already standard in all McStain homes was upgraded with new technology and products.

- Heating and cooling loads of the home were reduced by upgrading insulation in the shell of the house. The framing system provided insulation in corners and at wall intersections where typically multiple studs created a thermal bridge.

- Spray cellulose was used throughout the house. The cellulose material was 100 percent recycled newsprint and paper mixed with a non-toxic latex binder to create an infiltration-resistant barrier with a similar R-value to fiberglass. When compared with homes insulated with fiberglass, cellulose insulation resulted in a house that was 25 percent tighter.

- Tyvek™ house wrap added to the tight envelope and reduced infiltration while allowing moisture to escape. The net result was a reduction of air infiltration rates from conventional .5 air changes per hour to .12 air changes, a 75 percent improvement in performance.

- The orientation of the house was adjusted to provide optimal solar gain. The majority of the glazing was south facing, allowing for significant passive solar heat gain on cold winter days. This reduced the heating load by 30 percent.

- Low-E, argon-filled vinyl windows with an R-3.2 completed the package.

- The combination of the conservation package and the passive solar gain reduced the heating load by almost half. This was enough to eliminate the furnace altogether. The domestic hot water heater alone could provide heat to the house.

- Because the house was so tight, a Vent-Aire™ heat recovery ventilator (HRV) was used to provide fresh air. Working in conjunction with the HRV was a high-efficiency Nautilus natural gas water heater. The water heater was attached directly to the HRV, allowing hot water to flow into a fan-coil unit built into the ventilation unit.

Air drawn into the heat exchanger was circulated through the house like a typical forced air system. High returns on the south side of the house captured the solar gain, and the HRV recirculated it as well. By combining the air exchange with the heat recovery ventilator, a high level of energy efficiency was attained without a loss in occupant comfort. The Vent-Aire™ system recovered roughly 85 percent of exhaust air.

Improved Indoor Air Quality

A high-efficiency particulate air (HEPA) filter was installed to eliminate dust, dander, and airborne particles. Polluted air from the kitchen and bathrooms was circulated through the HRV system and replaced with fresh, filtered, heated, outdoor air. By continually exhausting stale indoor air and circulating fresh air, the house felt like a spring day in the coldest weather.

The Vent-Aire heat recovery ventilator as a substitute for a conventional furnace was a substantial step toward improving indoor air quality. To complement the HRV, several materials and finishes were selected for their low off-gassing quality.

In this category, McStain worked with David Adamson of Eco Build in Boulder to eliminate as many potential toxins as possible. Paint chosen for the house was Glidden's Spred 2000™ VOC-free interior paint. Non-toxic floor finishes were selected: naturally stain-resistant Image carpet made from recycled plastic bottles, natural linoleum manufactured with non-toxic natural ingredients by DLW, and a water based hardwood finish. All construction used solvent-free non-toxic Franklin adhesives.

Particleboard, which is common in new construction, was eliminated in the house because it off-gasses formaldehyde for years. Cabinetry was constructed of Medite II™ medium density fiberboard. Manufactured with a formaldehyde-free bonding agent, the off-gassing was eliminated.

Perhaps the simplest solution with the most dramatic results for improving indoor air quality was a garage fan that operated when the garage door opener was used. According to the EPA, the single biggest contributor to indoor air pollution is exhaust fumes emitted from cars, so the garage fan was an important choice.

Resource Conserving Building Materials

Materials were evaluated according to cost, availability, recycled content, environmental impact during manufacture, and maintenance requirements. McStain developed a materials palette that was easily adapted into production building.

Engineered wood products were chosen for constructing the Research House. Wood I-joists from Trus Joist International replaced 2x10 wood floor joists. Laminated veneer lumber was used in place of 2x12 structural beams. Louisiana Pacific was chosen for the reduced-formaldehyde, inner seal OSB, finger-jointed studs, and Fiberbond drywall. All framing on the Research House was done with 2x6 studs rather than the traditional 2x4s.

Thermo-Ply™ structural grade insulated sheathing made from 100 percent recycled material was used throughout. In addition to its recycled content, Thermo-Ply™ is 99 percent recyclable and is manufactured using only non-toxic bonding agents. For the exterior finish, siding made from 95 percent recycled material was selected. Banner Recycled Paints supplied exterior paint.

Instead of pressure treated lumber for the decking, McStain used Trex™ wood polymer composite deck material. Constructed from 100 percent recycled wood fiber and plastic, Trex™ decking offers a very long life, is 100 percent recyclable, and does not require painting or staining. Westile Feather Stone™ cement tile roofing was chosen for its durability, long-life, and low life-cycle costs. Completing McStain's commitment to resource efficiency, recycling was done on the construction site.

Conscious of the precious nature of water in the semiarid

Colorado landscape, McStain relied on xeriscaping where appropriate. Drought-tolerant native plants were chosen for tree and shrub groupings and some fescues were used for turf.

——— Greenlee Park ———

The Greenlee Park subdivision of the master-planned community of Indian Peaks in Lafayette, Colorado, demonstrates how the Research House innovations were translated into production building. The development opened in 1996, with several models

of town homes, carriage homes (small single family), and manor homes (duplexes). All homes within Greenlee Park are geared toward first-time buyers and alternative buyers (singles, single parents, and seniors). Prices range from $120,000 to $160,000 with finished square footage varying from 850 to 1650 plus unfinished basements.

The intention with Greenlee Park was to make environmentally responsible buildings affordable and aesthetically appealing. Materials and systems used in the Research House were adapted for use in this development. Some were eliminated because they were either too costly or unnecessary.

The standard **environmental package** in all Greenlee Park homes reflects the majority of the substitutions involved in the Research House. The Vent-Aire™ heat recovery ventilation system, spray cellulose insulation, double-pane, low-E, argon filled windows by Wenco and automatic dual set back thermostats comprise the core of the increased energy efficiency package.

Air quality is improved through reduced-formaldehyde OSB, Kwal EnviroKote™ paints, and solvent free non-toxic Franklin adhesives.

The list of **resource conserving building materials** is substantial: Louisiana Pacific I-joists and OSB, hardboard siding and exterior trim made from reconstituted wood fibers, Trex™ decking made from recycled wood fibers and plastic bags, finger-jointed studs, recycled cellulose insulation, and Shaw carpet made from recycled pop bottles.

On the whole, Greenlee Park offers the homebuyer the benefits of improved indoor air quality and increased energy efficiency. Given the high efficiency of the overall package, savings in heating costs quickly make up for the 1-1/2 percent increase in initial costs.

Many of these options are being investigated for other McStain developments. The manor and carriage homes in a Longmont subdivision are offered with an environmental eco-option that includes low-E glazing, evaporative cooler, 90 percent efficient gas forced-air furnace (an 80 percent efficient furnace is standard), ceiling fans, recycled content carpet, natural linoleum, Envirotec 2000™ adhesives, custom Medite II™ countertops, and compact fluorescent lighting.

——— Conclusion ———

The popularity of homes built by McStain Enterprises speaks to the rapidly-growing public interest in this type of production housing. McStain's on-going commitment to sustainable building practices for large-scale development provides an excellent model for other developers to emulate.

Behind-the-Walls Expo
Florida

Building an energy-efficient home is only half the battle. The most important aspect of the project is selling the home. Often that is left to realtors. It can cost time and money if the house sits on the market and the buyers are not given the information they need to make an informed purchase decision. That is where Philip Russell takes the initiative and markets his homes with the panache of Madison Avenue.

—— Consumer Education ——

In 1993 Russell began to educate the public and the trades in how to build energy efficient homes. He opened a house to the public and the trades at a time when most houses are the exclusive domains of plumbers, electricians, and carpenters. "The primary goal is to create consumer awareness," says Mick Donovan, Russell's General Manager. "The products are there to build better homes, but unless the consumer demands them, the builders are reluctant to use them."

The Behind-the-Walls Expo was a ten-day event with house tours, product exhibitions, barbecues, school field trips, and seminars for the public and the trades. From morning to night, special events were held for different groups. Over 640 people toured the house during the event. Gulf Power, the local utility, held a barbecue for staff, the press, and industry representatives. On the opening day, 100 third grade children toured the house. They left a "time capsule" of messages written on the Tyvek house wrap. "Saff the Erth," wrote one eight-year-old time traveler. "This house is Cool cause of insalation," wrote another. The kids spent hours touring the house and asking questions. Philip Russell gave the kids a special tour, explaining how houses are built and how construction differs from in the past. Bill Palmer from DuPont joined Russell and the kids. The two local TV stations featured the kids on the evening news.

——— Sponsors ———

The demonstration homes are made possible by contributions from major building industry corporations: Amoco, Carrier, GE, Honeywell, IBM, Pella, Trus Joist MacMillan, Sears, OCF are just a few of the 60 sponsors who have contributed to the success of the Behind the Walls Expo.

All of the sponsoring manufacturers and suppliers have booths and demonstrations scattered throughout the house. The house looks like a building products trade show. They have representatives to answer questions from the public. Most sponsors participate because they find demonstrable value in the public exposure to their products. Russell's quality and integrity have not been lost on marketing directors for some of the suppliers. "Philip is the reason we are doing this project. He is tenacious in his approach to building quality homes and in educating the public" says Bill McNeal of J.F. Day, of the Pella (window) Corporation.

The local utility, Gulf Power, used the event to kick off its Environmental Home Program. "Gulf Power believes in using natural resources wisely. We practice and teach energy conservation to our customers. We have hosted two Department of Energy programs to demonstrate burning coal more cleanly," says Steve Higgenbottom of Gulf Power. "We support two wildlife sanctuaries because we think environmental awareness and stewardship is the responsibility of business of all kinds. After all, we live here too. Florida is a beautiful place, and protecting that is important."

——— The House ———

The house in Pensacola has over 10,000 square feet under roof with 6000+ sq. ft. of living space. Yet it will only cost about $130 per month to heat and cool the house. The 2x6 construction is sheathed with Thermoply™, covered with Amoco foam board, and wrapped with Tyvek™, which helps to keep the load down. The R-value of the finished wall is 30. The ceiling has R=19 batts to code. The insulated fiberglass ductwork is laid over the batts and the whole ceiling is sprayed with another nine inches of loose fill fiberglass to create an R=40.

A radiant barrier under the roof sheathing and continuous ridge ventilation keeps unwanted heat from reaching the living space. The penetrations in the home are foamed to seal the cracks and penetrations in the shell. "Seal the house and mastic the ducts and you can save 20 percent of energy costs easily" says Mike Abbott of Energy Smart™.

Incorporating passive solar design features and a solar domestic hot water system further reduces the energy load. The hot water collectors are powered with a small photovoltaic cell on the roof that runs the pumps only when the sun is shining. Little additional back up electricity is needed in the sunny Florida coast climate.

The real winner in the energy package is the geothermal heat pump system. The closed loop system from Carrier uses state-of-the-art technology to provide an Energy Efficiency Ratio (EER) of 21.2. This is one of the highest possible ratings. The rating is achieved by drawing three-quarters of the energy for heating and cooling from 180 ft. deep borings adjacent to the house. The closed loop geothermal system is a two-way heat transfer mechanism. A small pump circulates a water solution in the pipe loop, and the heat is transferred to or extracted from the earth.

The water-to-air unit has a two-circuit design with dual compressors. If the load is small enough, only one compressor will respond. To improve performance, the blower motor is variable speed, only pushing as much air as is required. Excess heat is col-

lected by a tube-in-tube heat exchanger and directed to the domestic hot water tank to augment the solar system. The complete system provides comfort for about half the monthly cost of a typical air-to-air heat pump.

No detail is insignificant to Russell. He foams each wire penetration between stud cavities to prevent air movement. He runs two electrical circuits per room to reduce electro-magnetic fields in rooms. He installs heat recovery ventilation to maintain good indoor air quality.

Marketing

Once the Pensacola house was completed, Russell kept it open to the public for four months as a training center for builders and a showcase for homebuyers. During that time the house was filled with activity. Russell "co-partnered" with the Northwest Florida

Arts Council, an umbrella for the local symphony, museum, jazz groups, and galleries. The council sponsored jazz concerts and art exhibitions in the home that brought hundreds of people through the house. These events were in addition to public tours that included a film and demonstrations showing the features of the house. Other groups used the house for events. Each visitor was given a coded electronic card to run through a card reader for product information from sponsors on features of interest to them.

The whole marketing approach has set Russell apart from other builders in the area and has set a standard for creative home marketing. Builders from around the country have benefited from Russell's open approach in telling his story. He has been so besieged with requests for information on his construction practices that he created a video. He has sold over 5000 copies through word-of mouth and published articles. His book, *Energy-Smart Building for Increased Quality, Comfort, and Sales*, was published by Home Builder Press of the National Association of Home Builders.

"I don't mind if other builders copy what I am doing. If it saves energy and resources, its good for the country," admits Russell. "We build out of enjoyment and sincerity. That's why we do this stuff. Generations of people will own these houses. I build for them."

Dewees Island South Carolina

Dewees Island is a unique private island development off the coast of South Carolina. It was built on principles of **sustainable development**, one of the major selling points of the island.

The Dewees development was based on the belief that man and nature can coexist in a harmonious balance without negative impact. On the 1206 acre island, only 150 homes will be built. Sixty-five percent of the land is restricted from being developed at all, and 350 acres are given over as a wildlife refuge. The developers considered many environmental factors such as water quality, site selection, natural resource use, wildlife habitat, aesthetics, green building materials, and historical preservation.

───── Designing the Development ─────

John Knott is a visionary in sustainable development. After he and his design team performed in depth analyses of soils, topography, wetlands, flora, and fauna, they decided to concentrate island housing in the maritime forest. They designed the development to impact no more than 5 percent of the island. In doing this, the team incorporated green building practices such as passive solar heating and cooling, daylighting, capturing prevailing winds, construction waste management, and environmentally-sound building materials.

In the first year of work, Knott took the builders, trades contractors, and architects through 40 hours of seminars. In addition,

Knott educated Dewees residents. Homeowners were educated on composting, source reduction, reuse, and recycling. Knott says, "We started our own trade show for the community to exhibit building products and systems."

Builders and architects on Dewees are required to consider aesthetic features of the island when building new homes. Where vegetation is mature enough, the roofline of the home cannot exceed the height of the surrounding trees. And trees cannot be removed without a permit. Where vegetation is disturbed by construction, the area is then landscaped with indigenous plantings. Other attempts at increasing the beauty of the island include a whole island reforestation plan, planting wildflowers, and raised beach access paths which protect sensitive ecosystems.

Preserving Water

Efforts have been made to maintain water quality and to limit water use. In the homes, only water conserving plumbing fixtures are allowed, and all of the island's wastewater is treated in a state-of the-art absorption field. The only allowable irrigation is a combination of rainwater collection and below ground drip irrigation.

To control excess water and to preserve water quality, all roads are paved with sand to allow rainwater to infiltrate the water table. Natural features such as wetlands, oceanside dunes, and a salt marsh are managed to maintain their ecological integrity both as wildlife habitats and natural water purifiers. Ponds and swales increase the island's ability to handle excess water and to increase natural habitats.

——— Protecting Wildlife ———

Not only is Knott making sustainable decisions in the present, he is planning for the future health of the island ecosystem. In an effort to protect wildlife on the island, a comprehensive wildlife management plan addresses the island's flora and fauna. An Impoundment Management Plan was added in 1994. This plan provides strategies for controlling, monitoring, and/or enhancing the island habitat.
Managing and monitoring these habitats gives island ecologists insight into how to mitigate resident impact and promote proliferation of the species that inhabit the island.

—— Marketing the Community ——

When I asked Knott how he speaks of his vision to prospective buyers, he said: "I'm not sure we can communicate the magic of the island. We get visitors to experience it. You will find the accidental meeting place, a sense of surprise and discovery, and diversity throughout the community. Aesthetics and beauty are present in the buildings and landscape and in the expression of art in the community. The owners leave their mark by helping to build the community. As they experience attention to detail, they see the connection to nature and the beauty that comes from that."

—— The Magic of the —— Island Development

John Knott understands that magic is in short supply these days. He says, "Most neighborhoods are very sterile, disconnected from everything. Children and seniors are prisoners of the automobile and there is no real sense of community, so people aren't connected to one another. We've removed from our society the sense of adventure and discovery that used to be part of everyday life. We want to reestablish the opportunity to build our creativity and self-worth."

A desire to provide a sense of discovery and wonder for children and adults alike underlies the education and nature centers on the island. "Our staff environmentalists involve youngsters in collecting and analyzing environmental data, so kids take a real interest in the Island's research activities. Don't tell the kids, however (he winks and whispers) . . . we don't want them to know they're learning something as they have fun!" Knott says.

Marketing for Dewees Island invites people to be part of something special. They are asked to remember nature experiences which left an indelible mark on them as children and encourages them to provide that same magical experience for their own children or grandchildren.

Creating a Sense of Place

"A lot of times we think we are in the business of sticks and bricks, but we're not," remarks Knott. As builders we are so inundated with everything else we need to do, and we feel beat up all the time, so it is tough enough to build the house, let alone think about the community.

"When we create a place, it is as important to understand the client and serve their needs, as well as to serve the needs of the larger community in which the user participates. It is a connected system.

"If you understand that you are marketing an environment and a community, and you understand what the components are that make it a whole place, then when people come to see your home, in that place they will be very excited about it, because they are very excited about that place.

"When I think of the house itself, I believe that we, as builders, have got to remember that we are the professionals. Put the face of your children on the home that you are building and say, is this a place that I want my children to grow up in? Is this a place I want my adult children to buy and have as their first home? Would I feel confident in the healthfulness of that environment? Would I feel confident that they aren't throwing money down the drain? Am I creating the best environment I can with sensible use of resources that generate lower costs and improve durability for them? If we think that way, we will pull ourselves out of a lot of building habits we've gotten into over the last 30 or 40 years and we will build everything with them in mind."

The magic of Dewees is based on the magic of nature herself. Sustainable design is nothing more than remembering how we used to live in harmony with nature. Dewees has struck a chord with its market. It has attracted buyers who remember a sense of community, a sense of "place" where generations can follow each other—in a place called home. Dewees may be unique in its setting, but the principals that have made it such a success in the market today are transferable to any new development. If we build every home for our children, we will build a future in which they can flourish.

Appendices

There are vast resources available to green builders. Often, finding them is a challenge. This will serve as a "one stop shop" for how to learn more and who to contact for further information.

Appendix A: Green Builder Programs - Many programs are available to help a builder go green. The Denver Metro "Built Green" program, targeted at production builders has been enthusiastically received by the local market and has set a national precedent. Austin, Texas has the oldest program in the country and is exemplary in creating market demand for builders. Summaries of several HBA programs and their checklists have been included in this chapter.

Appendix B: Resources - A suggested green building reading list, contact information the HBA green builder programs, web sites, organizations, and companies.

Appendix C: Bibliography - A list of sources cited in the text, arranged by chapter.

Appendix A
Green Builder Programs

A wide variety of green builder programs exist to help you gain visibility and to assist you in selling your homes. Six Home Builder Associations around the country are specifically designed to help builders market their green homes. Others are in development and may be in place by the time this book is published. In addition, states and municipalities are developing programs to guide architects, builders, and homebuyers in defining green building in their market.

The benefit of using an existing program checklist is to get the whole picture of green building. Each program has a slightly different focus so four program checklists have been included for reference. Experiment with the different programs to see how your buildings compare with what the program certifies. Even though the Austin, Texas, program is a city-utility-based program, it is the original and the most diverse in content.

The National Association of Home Builders Research Center identified the program contents for six HBA programs. The following material is from their study, "A Guide to Developing Green Builder Programs," by Peter Yost. It provides an overview of how the programs operate and the types of marketing assistance they conduct. The NAHB-RC Guide is very useful for you to work with your local HBA to set up a program.

For a copy contact: NAHB-RC, 400 Prince George's Boulevard, Upper Marlboro, MD 20774.

—— Summary Profiles of Six HBA Programs ——

Program Titles:
- City of Austin, TX Green Builder Program
- Metropolitan Denver HBA "Built Green" Program
- HBA of Central New Mexico Green Builder Program
- Build a Better Kitsap,
- Build a Better Clark County
- Suburban Maryland HBA

Program Membership: 10 - 50 (Builders)

Program Costs:
- Builders (HBA members): $0 - $295 annual membership, $0 - $75 per project fee
- Associates (HBA members): $0 - $295

Program Coverage:
- Primarily residential builders, some cover major remodeling, one covers land developers separately

HBA Program Development Partners:
- Four partner with various local government agencies, one with private industry, and one with no partners

Sponsors Or Associate Members:
- Non-building members: architects, subcontractors, building suppliers, lenders

Methods Of Certification:
- Most have builder pledged, self-certification, some have or are developing a random check system

Resources:
- Builder Handbook Yard Signs, Window Decals
- Builder Resource Directory Program Newsletter
- HBA Resource Library Web Site
- Builder Plaque HBA local media promotion
- Homeowner Certificates Camera-ready Artwork
- Builder Fact Sheets Homeowner Manuals
- Builder Training Consumer Brochures

Education/Training:
- Initial orientation
- Regular training seminars
- "Green Builder University"

Builder/Consumer Surveys:
- Builder member, home buyers, general consumer phone and mail surveys
- Builder and homebuyer focus groups

Other Activities:
- Newsletter
- Awards Program
- Parade of Homes
- School "Green Building" Program

Program Structures:
- Austin - Four rating levels with 170 items total, 18 items required for all levels
- Denver - One level with 136 items total, 1 energy requirement
- Kitsap - Three levels with 85 items total, 5 items required for all levels
- Central New Mexico - Four levels with 70 items total, increasing requirements at each level
- Suburban Maryland - Two program sections, both with one level: builders have 39 items total, developers have 33 items total

Unique Features:
- Austin - city developed and administered program, free program, very detailed resource book, community category including land development issues
- Denver - nearly total builder flexibility with program items, extensive marketing and education partnership with state government., HBA resource library, nearby Boulder city program
- Kitsap - point weighting for items, handbook with carefully linked content areas and local resources, significant homeowner component, upcoming focus on remodeling
- Central New Mexico - "write-in" option for builder flexibility, spot checking for compliance, item distribution required at all levels, private program development partners
- Suburban Maryland - separate program sections for builders and developers, no partners–a stand alone HBA program, review board and site visits

Information characterizing the programs was obtained during 1998. Contact each HBA for the most current information on their program.

———— HBA of Central New Mexico ————

Green Builder Program

On a 4 Star rating system, the number of stars and then an equal sign indicates the number of points required to reach a given rating. (Example: *** = 4; To achieve a three star rating four points must be completed.)

Green Builder Home Checklist

Please check all items which apply

(Number of points are in parentheses)

Water Conservation (* = 4; ** = 4; *** = 6; **** = 6)

___ (1) Toilets that are 1.6 gallons per flush or less

___ (1) Shower heads that are 2.5 gallons per minute

___ (1) Faucets that are 2.0 gallons per minute

___ (1) Dishwasher with a water conservation cycle

___ (2) A hot water recirculation pump and timer

___ (1) Clothes washer with a water conservation cycle

___ (1) Landscaping: Full compliance with Landscaping and Waste Water Standards. (See Resource Guide for specifics)

___ (2) Centrally located hot water heater

___ (2) A pedal faucet controller

___ (2) Recirculation Pump for Hot Water Heater with Timer

___ (4) Disruption of no more than 50% of the natural state of the lot___ (4) Grey Water recycling system

___ (4) Landscaping: 90% of the area to be landscaped shall utilize only medium and/or low water use plants with a "drip" or trickle irrigation system with automatic timer controls. Xeriscape landscaping is also allowed

Materials: Conservation and Content (* =4; ** = 6; *** = 8; **** = 10)

___ (1) Paints & Finishes that are Low VOC (Volatile Organic Compound)

___ (1) Expanded Polystyrene (EPS) Foam Insulation which does not contain chlorofluorocarbons (CFCs) or hydrochlorofluorocarbons (HCFCs) (ozone-depleting products)

___ (1 each) Materials that are identified as containing recycled-content, please list:

_____

_____

_____

___ (1 each) Materials that are engineered materials, please list:

_____

_____

_____

___ (1) Use of locally produced products, please list:

_____

_____

_____

___ (1) Concrete that contains at least 15% fly ash

___ (2) Centrally located Electrical Panel

___ (4) Home construction using substantial portion of: adobe, straw bale, tires or cans, please describe: _____

Solid Waste Reduction (* = 5; ** = 7; *** = 7; **** = 10)

___ (2) An in-home recycling center, i.e. 3 bin kitchen cabinet or center in garage

___ (1) Garbage disposal

___ (4) Recycle on-site framing lumber waste. (This item is required.)

___ (2) Recycle on-site cardboard waste

___ (1) Backyard compost center

___ (1) Recycle on-site excess carpet pad & metal

___ (2) Recycle sheet-rock

Energy Conservation (* = 7; ** = 13; *** = 19; **** = 24)

___ (2) Windows that have a total-unit R-Value of R1.92

___ (3) Windows that have a total-unit R-Value of R2.44

___ (4) Windows that have a total-unit R-Value of R2.7

___ (3) Cooling: Select 1

   a. Evaporative Cooler with Thermostat

   b. Premium evaporative cooler w/celdek single media rather than multiple aspen pads, i.e. "Master Cool" or "Ultra Cool"

   c. Central A/C with a minimum of SEER 10

___ (2) Heating: Select 1

   a. Gas HVAC unit, 90% efficiency or greater with a programmable thermostat

   b. Gas boiler system, minimum 80% efficiency or greater with a programmable thermostat

   c. Heat pumps require a minimum efficiency of 6.8 HSPF, programmable thermostat or outdoor thermostat required

   d. Radiant heat with a minimum of one thermostat per five hundred sq.ft

___ (2) Duct Standards: Select 1

   a. Ducts must be located within the conditioned space

   b. Taped with U.L. 181 tape. Or Sealed with latex, water-based mastic sealant; must be non-toxic & applied per manufacturer's specs

   c. Insulation should be R8 for homes with refrigerated air and R6 for homes with evaporative cooling and/or forced air heating

___ (1 each) Ceiling fans. (Up to a maximum of 3 points) # of Ceiling Fans: _____

___ (1) Water Heater that operates at a minimum .57EF (Efficiency Factor) for 30 gallon capacity, .55EF for 40 gallon and, .53 for 50 gallon

___ (1) Insulated Blanket/Wrap for Water Heater

___ (2) R38 Insulation in the ceiling

___ (2) In addition to the previously established Wall and Ceiling Insulation standards, full compliance with NAHB Thermal Performance Guidelines

___ (2) Insulation below heated slab with EPS (minimum R value of 2.5)

___ (1) Insulation for hot water lines to/from recirculation pump

___ (1) Fluorescent lighting in a minimum of 2 separate locations

___ (1) Programmable thermostat

___ (1) Gas or EPA certified wood burning fireplace if installed (gas logs, gas appliance)

___ (1) Insulate garage

___ (1) Install insulated garage door

___ (2) Compact fluorescent lights used in recessed lighting (per 10 fixtures, maximum 4 points allowed)

___ (2) Whole house fan system (one fan in the attic that draws air up and out)

___ (2) Extended shades or awnings over southern and western windows. (See Resource Guide glossary for design standard of "extended shading".)

___ (2) Radiant Floor Heating

___ (3) Built-in appliances must have operating cost in the lower 50% range of the Energy Guide Sticker

___ (3) Increase hot water heater to 90% efficiency

___ (4) Solar gain design, i.e. 11-25 SF of south-facing glass per 100 SF of space floor are

——— City of Austin ———

Green Building Program

Basic Requirements

(An astericsk [*] indicates materials supplied by the Green Building Program)

The city of Austin uses a five-star rating system. All stars require that the basic requirements be fulfilled, plus a certain number of points from the Point List. One Star = 40-59; Two Stars = 60-89; Three Stars = 90-129; Four Star = 130-179

A home must have the following measures to qualify for a rating:

Materials

___ One recycled-content material (minimum 50% recycled) See list

___ Recycling center in kitchen, pantry, or utility room

Energy

___ City of Austin Energy Code requirements met

> Note: Shading to Code may be accomplished by any of the 3 following measures:
>
> a. Solar screens with 0.50 shading coefficient, or 0.445 solar heat gain coefficient, or lower
>
> b. Glass with 0.50 shading coefficient, or 0.445 solar heat gain coefficient, or lower (low-E, tint, film)
>
> c. Shading of the glass by roof overhangs sized according to code

___ Efficient and effective cooling and dehumidification system

> a. Home designed and specified to allow a minimum 600 sq. ft. of living space per ton of cooling
>
> b. Cooling system sized by Manual J (or equivalent computer analysis), based on actual design,
>
> specifications, and orientation
>
> c. Installed cooling tonnage based on the Manual J or equivalent calculation (not to exceed one ton/600 sq. ft.)
>
> d. Duct installation to City of Austin Energy Code
>
> e. 12.0 SEER minimum cooling efficiency
>
> a GBP Cooling System Information and Maintenance* instructions presented to homeowner

___ 2 ceiling fans

Heath, Safety

___ City of Austin Building Code requirements met

___ Low-VOC (volatile organic compound) paints used (1998 standard: water-based paint VOC's not to exceed 150 grams per liter and solvent-based paint VOC's not to exceed 380 grams per liter)

___ No vapor barrier (including vinyl wallpaper) installed on inside of perimeter wall

___ GBP Indoor Humidity* information presented to homeowner

___ One-inch minimum pleated-media filter installed in heating and cooling system

___ Any chemical termite control used is pyrethroid or borate based

___ GBP Integrated Pest Management* information presented to homeowner

Water

___ GBP Lawn Care* information presented to homeowner

Checklist

(Number of points are in parentheses)

Energy: High quality mechanical systems, efficient equipment, reduced need for mechanical systems

Design

___ (3) Home designer is a member of the Green Building Program

___ (2) Design created by design team, including designer, builder, and mechanical contractor

___ (3) A mechanical plan has been made concurrently with, and is part of, the construction plans and specs

___ (4) Size: maximum 1200 sq. ft. for 2 bedroom home + 250 sq. ft. maximum for each additional bedroom

___ (2) House shaded on east and west by existing or planted shade trees (minimum 50% of wall is/will be shaded)

___ (2) Buffer spaces placed on at least 50% of west wall (e.g. garage, covered porch, closets)

___ (2) Operable thermal chimney / cupola / clerestory designed for stack effect

___ (3) Glass on east and west is limited to 25% of total wall area: wall area_____, glass area_____, E+W glass_____

___ (4) Passive solar heating design (in regard to minimum and maximum south-facing glass; overhang size) See instructions*

___ (4) Duct work is located within the thermal envelope (insulated space)

___ (2) Home design allows for a minimum of 700 sq. ft. of living space per ton of cooling;

___ (4) Or home design allows for a minimum of 800 sq. ft. of living space per ton of cooling

___ (1) Raised-heel truss / rafter construction to allow for increased insulation and ventilation

___ (1) Fireplace is sealed gas unit with outside combustion air; or house has no fireplace

___ (2) Washer and dryer are located outside the home's heated and cooled space

___ (2) Covered outdoor area such as porch or patio (minimum of 100 sq. ft.)

Thermal Envelope

___ (2) "Total fill" insulation in walls (e.g. wet-blown cellulose, BIBS, open-cell foam, cementitious foam), or wall is integrally insulated or requires no added insulation (e.g. ICF, SIPS, straw, earth)

___ (4) Blower door test performed by qualified technician results in range of 0.35-0.45 Air Changes per Hour

___ (2) Continuous ridge and soffit vents; or attic is included in heated and cooled space

___ (3) Roof radiant barrier

___ (2) No skylights (solar tubes okay; skylights into porches okay)

___ (2) Double pane windows

___ (2) Tile roof

___ (2) Light colored exterior walls

Heating, Cooling, Water Heating

___ (2) Ceiling fans in all main rooms and bedrooms (not required in dining rooms)

___ (1) Whole-house fan with insulated cover

___ (1) 13.0 SEER cooling equipment efficiency

___ (2) Or 14.0 SEER cooling equipment efficiency

___ (3) Or 15.0 SEER cooling equipment efficiency

___ (1) Programmable or set-back thermostat

___ (2) No main HVAC trunk lines made of flex duct and no flex duct take-offs over 10' long

___ (1) Ducts cut to exact length and supported to manufacturer's specs

___ (2) No turns in ductwork greater than 90 degrees

___ (2) 90 degree angles in rigid duct have turning vanes or long-radius curves; take-offs have air grabbers

___ (2) Air-balancing dampers installed at each start collar

___ (2) Supply registers sized to deliver calculated air flow, return air grill sized to accomodate the system's CFM

___ (1) System components matched according to ARI (Air-Conditioning & Refrigeration Institute)

___ (5) Direct duct pressure test with "duct blaster" by qualified technician results in 5% or less air leakage

___ (3) Energy recovery ventilator (Air Changes/Hour not to exceed 0.45 on blower door test)

___ (2) Water heater in best 25% on Energy Guide Label; or gas WH has Energy Factor of 0.59 or higher; or 0.57 plus heat-trap nipples

___ (2) Combo space / water heating system with minimum 76% Recovery Efficiency

___ (4) Solar domestic hot water or swimming pool heating system

Lighting, Appliances

___ (2) All recessed can lights are IC sealed type (performance-tested); or no recessed cans are installed

___ (2) Minimum of 3 light fixtures are provided with fluorescent lamps (compact or tube)

___ (1) Outdoor lights are fluorescent, motion detector, or photovoltaic

___ (4) Photovoltaics installed on home (garden pathway lights excluded)

___ (2) Installed appliances are efficiency-rated in best 25% on Energy Guide Label or if none installed, information about Energy Guide Labels is presented to homeowner

Materials: Durable, low-maintenance, engineered, certified, reused, recycled, recyclable, local, natural

Design, Structure

___ (1) Engineered floor trusses/joists

___ (1) Engineered roof trusses;

___ (2) Or alternate roof structure (e.g. I-beams, LVL, SIPS)

___ (2) Sill plate is alternative lumber (e.g. wood composite or plastic)

___ (1) Wall stud framing is on 24" centers (as Code allows);

___ (2) Or wall framing is by the "Optimum Value Engineering" method (as Code allows);

___ (3) Or wall system (exterior) is engineered or alternative type (e.g. SIPS, ICF, ACC, straw, earth)

Finish Materials

___ (2) Exterior wall finish is brick, stone, stucco, or cement-based (minimum 80%)

___ (2) Roofing has 40 year or more warranty

___ (2) Porch / deck flooring: lumber is reused, reclaimed, or alternative (e.g. wood composite, plastic lumber)

___ (2) Doors or cabinet wood is reused or local species (e.g. pecan, mesquite, Texas juniper)

___ (2) Trim is finger-jointed or engineered or MDF or reused or local species

___ (1) Recycled-content (50% or more content) or reused material (in addition to Basic Requirement choice: 1 point/material)

_____

_____

___ (3) Floor is durable material for minimum of 1/2 of all flooring (e.g. concrete, stone, brick, wood, ceramic tile)

___ (2) Structural floor is finish floor for minimum 1/3 of all floor (e.g. exposed concrete, single-layer wood)

___ (2) Flooring: natural fiber carpet (e.g. wool, jute, grass); linoleum (not vinyl); cork; bamboo; local species, or reused wood; or there is no carpet in the house

Excess Jobsite Resources

___ (2) Cut trees are reused, not sent to landfill (e.g. mulched)

___ (2) Wood scraps longer than 2 feet are reused/recycled

___ (2) Paper / cardboard packaging and aluminum cans are recycled (receptacles provided on jobsite)

___ (2) Metals are reused/recycled

___ (2) Excess building materials are reused, given/sold to salvage, or donated to Habitat for Humanity RE-store

Water: Conservation of all water; protection of water quality

Indoor

___ (1) Showerheads use no more than 2.0 gallons of water per minute (free from Water Conservation Dept.)

___ (3) Horizontal axis clothes washer

___ (1) Dishwasher uses no more than 7 gallons of water per load on normal cycle

___ (2) Water heater is located within 20' of dishwasher, clothes washer and baths it serves; or demand-type hot water recirculator is installed and all hot water lines are insulated to Austin code

Outdoor

___ (2) Existing natural vegetation is essentially retained on at least 50% of pervious cover area

___ (2) Turf grass/lawn does not exceed 50% of pervious cover area

___ (2) Turf grass/lawn in sunny areas is low-water variety (buffalo or common Bermuda); or there is no turfgrass

___ (1) At least 90% of plants, shrubs, and trees are selected from the City of Austin Xeriscape brochure list

___ (1) All planting beds are mulched to minimum 2" depth

___ (2) Dillo Dirt is used for soil amendment (6 cubic yards minimum per site)

___ (3) Landscape requiring watering has a minimum 6" of top soil (includes turfgrass areas)

___ (2) Gutters and downspouts installed and directed away from foundation to landscaping or catchment system

___ (4) Rainwater catchment system installed

___ (1) Irrigation system has

    a) a controller for 5-day programming

    b) multiple start times

    c) 2 or more independent programs

    d) manual flow control valves

    e) rain shut-off device, f) matched precipitation heads with head-to-head spacing

    g) check valves for heads on slopes, and h) an "as-installed" plan provided to homeowner

___ (1) Drip irrigation system for non-turf areas

Take both irrigation points if you have no turf and only natural vegetation/native plantings

___ (4) Greywater system

Health, Safety: Improved air quality: reduced humidity, dust mites, and harmful chemicals

Molds, Mites, Fibers

___ (3) HVAC filter is electronic (not electrostatic); or 4" or thicker pleated-media type; easily accessed

___ (3) No fiberglass fibers are exposed to the air stream in duct work. (Use metal or lined duct material.)

___ (2) Humidistat installed in home

___ (3) Central humidity control system in addition to cooling system (ERV with enthalpy qualifies)

___ (3) Exhaust fans installed and vented to outside for cooktop/stove and any room with tub or shower (whether or not room has an operable window)

___ (1) Laundry room exhaust fan installed, vented to outside (whether or not room has an operable window)

___ (2) Bathroom fan connected to timer or humidistat

___ (2) 60% or more of finish flooring is hard surface material (not carpet)

Chemical Outgassing

___ (1) Interior paint is super-low VOC (under 100 grams per liter);

___ (2) Or interior paint has no VOC's (under 10 grams per liter);

___ (3) Or interior paint is natural (plant-based); or has no biocides

___ (2) Cabinet, paneling, moulding and floor finishes are water-based

___ (2) Construction adhesives have no VOC's

___ (2) Formaldehyde-free or natural insulation–check Material Safety Data Sheet (MSDS)

___ (3) Formaldehyde-free MDF for all interior uses (Check MSDS)

___ (2) Lockable hazardous-material cabinet, sealed off from living space and attached garage, vented outside

___ (2) Organized house ventilation procedure/commissioning conducted prior to occupancy

Combustion Gases

___ (3) Garage has exhaust fan with timer; or is separate structure from house; or there is no garage

___ (1) No unvented gas logs (venting must be to outside of building shell)

___ (4) House passes combustion safety/backdraft test as performed by qualified technician

___ (1) Carbon monoxide detector installed EMF's

___ (1) EMF-reducing wiring methods (See instructions)

___ (1) Electrical main panel set ten feet or more away from bedrooms and areas of frequent occupancy

Integrated Pest Management

___ (1) Any wood used (e.g. siding, trim, structure) is at least 1 foot above soil

___ (1) Fill dirt at foundation beams in plastic sand bags (not paper); no wood, cardboard, or paper left in soil under or near foundation; "sono-tube" forms removed

___ (1) Exterior wood-to-concrete connections are separated by metal or plastic; or there are no wood concrete connections

___ (4) Wood framing treated with a borate product to a minimum of 3 feet above foundation; or sand or diatomaceous earth barrier termite control system; or structure is not made of wood

Community: Improved quality of life; improved community ties; reduced urban sprawl

General

___ (3) Remodeling of an existing structure

___ (2) Home has a front porch large enough for family to use (100 sq. ft. minimum)

___ (4) Site has more than one dwelling unit (e.g. duplex, condo, "granny flat")

___ (2) Street, electricity, water, wastewater have been in place for a minimum of 15 years

___ (4) Home is located in a Traditional Neighborhood Design or Small Lot subdivision

___ (2) Public transit is within a 10-minute walk

___ (2) A shopping area is within a 15-minute walk

___ (2) Subdivision is adjacent to, or has a hike and bike trail or green belt or park

___ (2) Backyard compost bin specified and provided (site-built or off-the-shelf)

___ (2) Trees to be saved are protected with fencing at the drip line

___ (2) Builder is member of Clean Builder Program or home owner is member of the City of Austin Solar Explorer

———— Metropolitian Denver HBA ————

Built Green Checklist

1999 Built Green of Colorado

The Checklist

I. Energy Requirement

(One of the following must be included in each home)

___ Home receives energy rating of at least four-star as certified by Energy Rated Homes of Colorado or,

___ Home meets CABO MEC 93

II. Land Use: Lot (Choose 2)

___ Trees and natural features on site protected during construction

___ Save and reuse all site topsoil

___ Home placement saves east and south lot areas for outdoor use

___ Home oriented on lot such that the long dimension faces within 30 degrees of south

III. Waste Management (Choose 1)

___ Built-in kitchen recycling center with two or more bins

___ Minimize job site waste by using materials wisely and prohibit burying construction waste

___ Recycle job site waste (>50%)

IV. Energy Use: Envelope (Choose 2)

___ South glass area is between 5-7% of total finished floor area

___ Advanced sealing package in addition to basic sealing practices (advanced package adds sealing at top and bottom plates, corners and between cavities at penetrations)

___ Provide south roof area designed for future solar collector use (20 degrees of south)

___ Home designed for passive solar heating (>20%)

___ Energy heels of 6" or more on trusses

___ Two-foot overhang, between one and two feet above south windows

___ Blower door test with 0.35 ACH or less

___ House is wrapped with an exterior air infiltration barrier to manufacturer's specifications

___ House meets EPA 5-Star Program Standards

V. Energy Use: Mechanical (Choose 4)

___ Furnace centrally located, all duct runs reduced as much as possible

___ No ducts in outside walls or attics unless ducts have minimum R-13 value

___ Thermostat with on switch for furnace fan to circulate air

___ Two properly supported ceiling fan prewires

___ Sealed-combustion gas fireplace or sealed wood-burning fireplace or stove with outside combustion air

___ Setback thermostat

___ Furnace ductwork joints sealed with low toxic mastic

___ Whole house fan installed

___ Return-air ducts in every bedroom

___ 90% or higher energy efficiency furnace

___ Active solar heating system (solar fraction >20%)

___ Two or more thermostats controlling separate heating and cooling zones from a single furnace (not an attic furnace)

___ Geothermal heating, cooling and water heating system

VI. Energy Use: Indoor Air Quality (Choose 2)

___ Sealed-combustion furnace or boiler

___ Sealed-combustion domestic water heater

___ Exhaust fan in garage on timer or wired to door opener

___ Heat recovery ventilator or air-to-air heat exchanger

___ Radon mitigation installed or vent pipe laid under slab for retrofit

___ Mechanical room enclosed and insulated to R-11

___ Provide range hood vented to outside

___ Furnace and/or duct-mounted electronic air cleaner or HEPA filter

___ House meets American Lung Association Health House Standards

VII. Energy Use: Water Heating Systems (Choose 2)

___ Gas water heater with energy factor of 0.60 or greater

___ Insulate hot water pipes to R-6 in unconditioned spaces

___ Water heater within 20 pipe feet of dishwasher and clothes washer

___ Insulate all hot water lines to all locations to R-6

___ Rough-in for future solar hot water heating

___ Gas water heater with insulating blanket installed to manufacturer's specifications

___ Insulate hot and cold water pipes 3 feet from the hot water heater

___ Solar water heating system

VIII. Energy Use: Appliances (Choose 2)

___ Dishwasher with energy saving cycle

___ Gas clothes dryer with electronic ignition gas range, cooktop and/or oven with electronic ignition

___ Refrigerator less than $66 estimated annual electric cost per year

___ If appliances are not included, a list of energy efficient appliances is provided

___ Provide gas rough-in for clothes dryer, range, cooktop and/or oven when those appliances are not included with the home

___ Solar electric system provides 20% or more of the home's electricity

IX. Energy Use: Lighting (Choose 2)

___ Light-colored interior walls, ceiling and soffit

___ Light-colored carpet

___ Furnish four compact fluorescent light bulbs to owners

___ Halogen lighting substituted for incandescent down-lights

___ Extended-life incandescent bulbs greater than 2000 hrs (e.g., traffic signal bulbs)

___ No can lights in insulated ceiling or Insulation Contact-Rated (IC Rated) can lights are used

___ No can lights used in insulated ceiling or air-tight can lights are used

___ Solar-powered walkway or outdoor area lighting

X. Materials: Structural Frame (Choose 3)

___ Large dimension solid lumber (2x10 or greater) avoided in floors and roofs wherever possible

___ Dimensional lumber from 3rd party certified sustainably harvested sources

___ Engineered wood "I" joists used for floors

___ Trusses or "I" joists used for roofs

___ Structural insulated panels used for walls or roofs

___ Reinforced cementitious foam-formed walls using flyash concrete

___ Engineered lumber products for beams, joists or headers

___ Reduced framing package (24" O.C. studs at interior non-bearing walls, and 3 stud corners)

___ Finger-jointed plate material

___ Finger-jointed studs or engineered stud material

___ Engineered alternatives to wood framing

___ Outdoor structures, decking and landscaping materials made from pressure treated engineered lumber or non-CCA (chromated copper arsenate) dimensional lumber

___ Outdoor structures, decking and landscaping materials made from recycled materials

___ Outdoor structures, decking and landscaping materials made from 3rd party certified sustainably harvested lumber

XI. Materials: Foundation (Choose 1)

___ Non-asphalt based damp proofing (seasonal application)

___ Regionally produced block or brick

___ Western coal flyash concrete (minimum 15%, seasonal application)

___ Frost-protected shallow foundation

___ Aluminum foundation forms used

___ Rigid insulation forms that provide permanent insulation to the foundation

___ Insulated foundation with rigid R-10 foam insulation to footer

XII. Materials: Sub-Floor (Choose 1)

___ Urea formaldehyde-free subfloor and underlayment material

___ Oriented strand board (OSB) made from fast growth material

___ Recycled-content underlayment

XIII. Materials: Doors (Choose 2)

___ No Lauan doors (tropical hardwood)

___ Exterior doors insulated to R-5, or greater

___ Reconstituted or recycled-content doors (hardboard) with least toxic binders

___ Solid, domestically grown interior wood panel doors

XIV. Materials: Finish Floor (Choose 2)

___ Recycled-content carpet pad

___ Recycled-content carpet (tacked not glued)

___ Natural linoleum with low toxic adhesives or backing

___ Ceramic tile installed with low toxic mastic and grout

___ Recycled-content ceramic tile

___ Natural material carpet (domestic cotton, wool) tacked not glued

___ Domestic wood flooring made from 3rd party certified sustainably harvested sources

XV. Materials: Exterior Walls (Choose 2)

___ Recycled-content sheathing (minimum 50% pre- or post-consumer) or OSB

___ Reconstituted or recycled-content siding (minimum 50% pre- or post-consumer)

___ Regionally produced brick

___ Indigenous stone

___ Natural stucco and/or synthetic plaster

___ Cementitious siding

___ Reconstituted or recycled-content fascia, soffit or trim (minimum 50% pre- or post-consumer)

___ Molded cementitious "stone"

___ R-3.5 or better-insulated exterior wall sheathing

XVI. Materials: Windows (Choose 2)

___ Windows double glazed with 1/2" airspace

___ Finger-jointed wood windows

___ Low-E windows NFRC rated at u=0.37 or lower

___ Exterior environmental/insulated window coverings

___ No metal-frame windows in house, including basements

XVII. Materials: Cabinetry And Trim (Choose 1)

___ Any exposed particleboard is painted with water-based sealer inside cabinets, underside of countertops

___ Tropical hardwood trim or cabinets only if from 3rd party certified sustainably manageable forests

___ Finger-jointed trim

___ On-site application of cabinet finishes done with least toxic finishes

___ Domestic hardwood trim

___ Cabinets made with formaldehyde-free particleboard or MDF (medium density fiberboard) or recycled agricultural product

XVIII. Materials: Roof (Choose 1)

___ Recycled-content roof material

___ Minimum 30-year roofing material including concrete, slate, clay, composition, metal or fiberglass

XIX. Materials: Finishes and Adhesives (Choose 1)

___ Paints and finishes that have minimal VOC content. Standard is less than 250 grams/liter of VOCs

___ Paints or finishes with recycled-content

___ Only low toxicity, low solvent adhesives used throughout

___ Water-based urethane finishes on wood floors

___ Water-based lacquer finishes on woodwork

XX. Materials: Insulation (Choose 1)

___ Recycled-content (minimum 25%) insulation

___ Home has wet blown wall insulation such as cellulose or fiberglass

___ Cellulose insulation with UL-rated fire retardant

___ HCFC-free rigid foam insulation

___ Formaldehyde-free insulation

___ Non-toxic spray foam insulation

XXI. Water (Choose 1)

___ Permeable materials (40% of areas for all walkways, patios and driveways)

___ Grass that uses less water such as blue gramma or fescue in turf areas

___ Xeriscape that is more than 60% of non-paved area

___ Rainwater recovery from roof for watering

___ Xeriscape with native drought resistant plants

___ Provide a list of native drought resistant plants to homebuyers

___ 1.5 gpm faucets in bathrooms, installed to manufacturer's specifications

___ 2.0 gpm faucets in kitchen, installed to manufacturer's specifications

___ Front loading, horizontal axis, clothes washer

___ Passive or on-demand hot water deliver system installed at farthest location from water heater

———— Build A Better Clark County ————

Home Builder Self-Certification Checklist

Check items you will be including in this project
to qualify for a Build A Better Clark star rating

Requirements to Qualify at 1-Star Level

(All * items plus orientation):

___ Attend a Build A Better Clark Program
  Orientation (one time only)

___ Section 1: Build to "Green" codes/regulations

___ Prepare a job-site recycling plan

___ Use at least one recycled-content building
  product

___ Provide a "Homeowner's Kit"

Requirements to Qualify at 2-Star Level

(50 points minimum):

___ Meet 1-Star requirements

___ Earn 8 points from Section 2

___ Earn 12 points from Section 3

___ Earn 6 points from Sections 4, 5, 6, 7, and 8

___ Attend a BBC-approved workshop within past
  12 months

Requirements to Qualify at 3-Star Level

(90 points minimum):

___ Meet 2-Star requirements plus an additional 40
  points

___ Attend a BBC-approved workshop within past
  12 months prior to certification

Section One: Build to Green Codes/Regulations

___ (*) Meet Washington State Energy Code

___ (*) Meet Washington State Ventilation/Indoor
  Air Quality Code

___ (*) Meet Washington State Water Use
  Efficiency Standards

Section Two: Treat Site Appropriately

Site Protection

(Number of points are in parentheses)

___ (1) Install temporary erosion control devices

___ (1) Stabilize disturbed slopes

___ (1) Install sediment traps

___ (1) Save & reuse all topsoil

___ (1) Balance cut and fill

___ (1) Wash out concrete trucks in slab or pave-
  ment sub-base areas

___ (1) Limit impervious surfaces to 3,000 sq. ft

___ (1) Set aside at least 20% of site that will not
  be cleared or graded

___ (1) Use low-toxic landscape materials and
  methods

___ (1) Use less toxic form releasers

___ (2) Do not leave any portion of site bare after
  construction is complete

___ (2) Replant or donate removed vegetation

___ (3) Grind landclearing wood & stumps for
  reuse

___ (3) Preserve existing native vegetation as landscaping

Site Design

___ (1) Provide rear access off alley for multi-
  family housing

___ (2) Provide a front porch

___ (2) Recess garage to behind front of house

___ (1) Provide a rear garage with alley access

___ (2) Provide an accessory dwelling unit

___ (3) Use permeable options for driveways,
  walkways, patios & parking areas

___ (3) Build on an infill lot

___ (5) Build in a Build A Better Clark certified
  development

_____ Subtotal for Section Two

Section Three: Reduce/Reuse/Recycle

Reduce

___ (1) Use standard building sizes in design

___ (1) Use quality tools and clean thoroughly
  between uses

___ (1) Set up labeled bins for different sized nails,
  screws, etc.

___ (1) Provide weather protection for stored
  materials

___ (1) Use drywall stops or clips for backing

___ (1) Use two-stud corners

___ (1) Use insulated headers

___ (1) Use ladder partitions on exterior walls

___ (2) Create detailed take-off and provide as cut
  list to framer

___ (2) Use suppliers who use reusable or recyclable packaging

___ (2) Use central cutting area or cut packs

___ (3) Require subcontractors to participate in
  waste reduction efforts

___ (3) Limit project size to under 1,800 sq. ft

Reuse

___ (1) Use reusable supplies for operations

___ (1) Reuse building materials

___ (1) Reuse dimensional lumber

___ (1) Sell or give away wood scraps

___ (1) Sell or donate reusable items from your job

___ (1) Move leftover materials to next job or provide to owner

___ (2) Purchase used building materials for your job

Recycle

___ (1) Recycle wood scrap

___ (1) Recycle cardboard

___ (1) Recycle metal scraps

___ (1) Recycle paint

___ (2) Recycle drywall

___ (3) Recycle asphalt roofing

___ (3) Recycle concrete/asphalt rubble

___ (*) Prepare a job-site recycling plan and post on site

_____ Subtotal for Section Three

Section Four: Purchase Resource-Efficient Products

___ (1) Use drywall with recycled-content gypsum

___ (1) Use recycled-content insulation

___ (1) Use resource-efficient carpet and/or padding

___ (1) Use recycled or "reworked" paint

___ (1) Use resource-efficient siding

___ (1) Use flyash in concrete

___ (1) Use recycled-content vinyl flooring

___ (1) Install materials with longer life-cycles

___ (1) Use finger-jointed wood products

___ (1) Use engineered structural products

___ (2) Use structural panel systems

___ (2) Use recycled concrete, glass cullet, or asphalt for base or fill

___ (3) Use recycled-content ceramic tile

___ (3) Use linoleum, cork, or bamboo flooring

___ (3) Use recycled-content plastic lumber

___ (3) Use re-milled salvaged lumber

___ (3) Use sustainably produced, certified wood

___ (3) Use salvaged or recycled-content masonry

___ (*) Use at least one recycled-content building product

_____ Subtotal for Section Four

Section Five: Maximize Energy

___ (1-10) Improve energy efficiency of building components prescribed by code

___ (1-10) Improve energy efficiency of building components affecting code performance

___ (1) Optimize hot water heating system (beyond code)

___ (1) Provide an outdoor clothesline

___ (1) Install timers for bathroom fans

___ (1) Install lighting dimmers, timers, and/or motion detectors

___ (2) Use compact fluorescent lighting

___ (2) Use light tubes for natural lighting and to reduce electric lighting

___ (2) Optimize air sealing techniques

___ (2) Use blown-in insulation

___ (2) Perform blower door test

___ (2) Install tankless (instantaneous) water heaters at taps

___ (2) Centrally locate furnace and hot water heater

___ (2) Orient building to make the best use of passive solar

___ (3) Install air-to-air heat exchanger

___ (3) Use building & landscaping plans that reduce heating/cooling loads naturally

_____ Subtotal for Section Five

Section Six: Promote Good Air Quality and Health

___ (1) Use improved air filters

___ (1) Supply workers with VOC-safe masks

___ (1) Install CO detector

___ (1) Exhaust central vacuum to outside; install equipment in garage

___ (2) Use low-VOC, low-toxic, water-based paints, sealers, finishes, or solvents

___ (2) Use low-VOC, low-toxic, water-based grouts, mortars, or adhesives

___ (2) Use less polluting insulation products

___ (2) Use foil-covered external insulation on metal ducting

___ (2) Install exhaust fans in rooms where office equipment is used

___ (2) Take measures during construction operations to avoid moisture problems later

___ (2) Take measures to avoid problems due to construction dust

___ (2) Design buildings to keep water out and off

___ (2) Create an "oasis" in family bedrooms

___ (3) Install sealed combustion heating and hot water equipment

___ (3) Reduce sources of interior formaldehyde

___ (3) Use low-toxic or less allergen-attracting carpets

___ (3) Limit use of carpet to one-third of home's square footage

___ (3) Provide balanced or slightly positive indoor pressure using controlled ventilation

___ (3) If providing central heating and cooling, install whole house dehumidification

___ (3) Optimize air distribution system

___ (3) Meet code req.'s for higher risk radon counties

___ (10) Certify house under the American Lung Association's Health House Advantage Program

_____ Subtotal for Section Six

Efficiency Section Seven: Manage Hazardous Waste Properly

___ (1) Use less or non-toxic cleaners

___ (1) Use water-based paints instead of oil-based paints

___ (1) Reduce hazardous waste through good housekeeping

___ (2) Reuse spent solvent for cleaning

___ (2) Recycle used antifreeze, oil, oil filters, and paint at appropriate outlets

___ (2) Dispose of non-recyclable hazardous waste at legally permitted facilities

_____ Subtotal for Section Seven

Section Eight: Promote Responsible Operations & Maintenance

___ (1) Install environmentally friendly water filter at sink

___ (1) Use drought-tolerant landscaping

___ (1) Provide homeowner with a compost bin

___ (1) Avoid solid fuel appliances

___ (2) Install extra-efficient domestic appliances

___ (2) Build recycling area into residence

___ (2) Build a lockable storage closet for hazardous household products

___ (3) Install high-efficiency irrigation system

___ (3) Provide a rainwater collection system for irrigation

___ (*) Provide a "Homeowner's Kit"

_____ Subtotal for Section Eight

_____ Total Points for Project

Program Level Obtained (circle one):

1-Star * 2-Star ** 3-Star *

Appendix B
Resources

There are vast resources available to green builders. Often, finding them is the problem. This will serve as a "one stop shop" for how to learn more and who to contact for further information.

Books & Publications

Architect's Energy Guide to Energy-Efficient Commercial Buildings
by Kelly A. Karmel, AIA, 1999
The American Institute of Architects, Colorado Chapter
1526 Fifteenth Street
Denver, CO 80202
A road map for energy efficient design, this book translates energy guidelines from components, into design processes.

Consumer Guide to Home Energy Savings
by Alex Wilson and John Morrill
American Council for an Energy-Efficient Economy (ACEEE)
1001 Connecticut Avenue, NW, Suite 801
Washington, DC 20036
Tel: (202)429-0063
Fax: (202) 429-0193
E mail:
ace3pubs@ix.netcom.com
Web site: aceee.org
Updated periodically with model numbers of the most efficient appliances (heating, kitchen, laundry, air conditioning). Information on selecting energy-efficient equipment and improving the performance and efficiency of older equipment.

The Ecology of Commerce
by Paul Hawken, 1993
HarperCollins Publishers, Inc.
10 East 53rd Street
New York, NY 10022
A re-envisioning of the way we do business in which, "every act is inherently sustainable and restorative."

Environmental Building News
Editor: Alex Wilson
Environmental Building News
28 Birge Street
Brattleboro, VT 05301
Tel: (800) 861-0954
Fax: (202) 429-0193

E mail:
ace3pubs@ix.netcom.com
Web site: www.aceee.org
EBN is a monthly newsletter featuring news, reviews, and feature articles on all aspects of environmentally sustainable design and construction. They are the best source for ongoing green building information. They also have searchable CD ROMs that contain all past issues.

EBN Product Catalog
Environmental Building News, 1998
28 Birge Street
Brattleboro, VT 05301
Tel: (800) 861.0954
Fax: (802) 257-7304
E mailebn@abuild.com
Web site: www.ebuild.com
Jointly published by What's Working and EBN, the comprehensive catalog of environmental product literature and references for 1200 building products provides both generic product information and specific product manufacturer listings.

Efficient Wood Use in Residential Construction: A Practical Guide to Saving Wood, Money, and Forests
by Anne Edminster and Sami Yassa, 1998
Natural Resources Defense Council, 40 West 20th Street
New York, NY 10011-4211
Tel: (212) 727-2700
Fax: (212) 727-1773
Web site: www.nrdc.org
A handbook for increasing the efficient use of wood in residential design and construction. Each chapter presents a wood-efficient strategy and then is divided into three categories: the bottom line, practical considerations, resources.

Environmental Resource Guide
Editor: Joseph Emkin, 1997
John Wiley & Sons
Detailed material assessments based on a modified life-cycle assessment methodology. Includes application reports and case studies.

Exemplary Home Builder's Field Guide
by Joseph Lstiburek, Building Science Corporation, 1994
The definite handbook for building safe, healthy, comfortable, durable, and energy-efficient homes. Organized for easy access and illustrated with 140 detailed construction drawings, it provides guidance and instruction on every phase of home-building from site planning to materials selection.

A Guide to Developing Green Builder Programs
By NAHB Research Center
400 Prince George's Boulevard
Upper Marlboro, MD 20774
A comprehensive study of the six home builder programs currently in place across the nation. Includes step-by-step how-to's on starting a green builder program and checklists from existing programs.

Green Building Advisor: Defining the Future of Environmentally Responsible Design
Center for Renewable Energy and Sustainable Technology, 1998
Available from:
E Build, Inc.
122 Birge Street, Suite 30
Brattleboro, VT 05391
Web site: www.ebuild.com
A combination of a CD-ROM and User Manual present an interactive approach to green

building design and education aimed at changing the way people think about and design buildings.

Green Development: Integrating Ecology and Real Estate
by Rocky Mountain Institute, Alex Wilson, 1998
published by John Wiley & Sons
Rocky Mountain Institute
1739 Snowmass Creek Road
Snowmass, CO 81654-9199
Tel: (970) 927-3851
Fax: (970) 927-4178
E mail: general@rmi.org
Web site: www.rmi.org
Covers all aspects of ecologically sensitive development, with real-world examples based on 80 case studies.

Handbook of Sustainable Building: An Environmental Preference Method for Selection of Materials for Use in Construction and Refurbishment
by David Anink, Chiel Boonstra, John Mak, 1996
James & James (Science Publishers) Ltd.
Waterside House
47 Kentish Town road
London NWI 8NZ, UK
Tel: +44 171 284 3833
Fax: +44 171 284 3737
This handbook aims to clarify the environmental choices facing designers when deciding on appropriate components and materials. It has an easy to use format which puts the most preferable products on the far left and the products which are not recommended on the far right.

Healthy By Design: Building & Remodeling Solutions for Creating Healthy Homes
by David Rousseau, James Wasley, 1997
Hartely & Mark Publishers
P.O. Box 147
Point Roberts, WA 98291
Tel: (800) 277-5887
Fax: (604) 738-1913
E mail: hartmark@direct.ca
Features a discussion of indoor pollutants and their sources, case studies of healthy and energy efficient homes, and

construction details conducive to healthier homes.

The Healthy House, 3rd Edition: How to Buy One, How to Cure a Sick One, How to Build One
By John Bower, 1997
The Healthy House Institute thoroughly researched materials and construction systems for improved indoor air quality.

Improving Energy Efficiency in Apartment Buildings
By John DeCicco, Rick Diamond, Sandra Nolden, Janice DeBarros, and Tom Wilson
Forward by Stephen Morgan.
This book reviews building characteristics, energy use, and barriers to conservation in existing five-or-more unit multi-family housing, and presents an up-to-date overview of approaches for audit and retrofit, energy-saving technology, conservation programs, evaluation, and financing strategies.

Mid-Course Correction Toward a Sustainable Enterprise: The Interface Model
By Ray C. Anderson, 1998
The Peregrinzilla Press
Order From: Chelsea Green Publishing Company
An astounding personal account of a CEO's mission to transform his carpet manufacturing company into a model of sustainability.

The Natural Home: Living the Simple Life
By Tricia Foley, 1995
Clarkson N. Potter, Inc.
201 East 50th Street
New York, NY 10022
A guide to decorating your home with simple, aesthetically pleasing, and environmentally sound designs.

Operating Manual for Spaceship Earth
By R. Buckminster Fuller, 1969
Simon and Schuster
Rockefeller Center
1230 Avenue of the Americas
New York, NY 10020
A primer in Fullerian thinking. Best place to start for understanding Bucky Fuller's thinking

and the future of the planet.

Our Ecological Footprint: Reducing Human Impact on the Earth
By Mathis Wackernagel and William Rees, 1996
New Society Publishers,
P.O. Box 189
Gabriola Island, B.C.
Canada VOR 1XO
Provides graphic and understandable illustrations of complex concepts such as carrying capacity, sustainablity, resource use and waste disposal, etc. A vital resource for community activists and planners.

Recyclying Resource Catalog
Integrated Solid Waste Management Offices
City of Los Angeles, Department of Public Works
433 Spring Street
5th Floor, MS 944
Los Angeles, CA 90013
Tel: (213) 847.1444
Fax: (213) 847-3054
E mail: ISWM@san.ci.la.ca.us
Web site: www.ci.la.ca.us
A recycling tool kit for architects, construction specifiers, contractors, governmental agencies, and others interested in recycling and buying recycled-content products.

Reducing Home Building Costs with OVE Design and Construction
NAHB Research Center, Inc.
400 Prince George's Blvd.
Upper Marlboro
MD, 20772-8731
Tel: (301) 249-4000
Fax: (301) 547-2604
E mail: lbowles@nahbrc.org
Web site: www.nahbrc.org
A book on how to design and build housing using optimum value engineering, which reduces material quantities used while increasing ease of construction.

A Reference Guide to Resource Efficient Building Elements, 6th Edition
Compiled and wirtten by: Steve Loken, Rod Miner, & Tracy Mumma, 1997
Center for Resourceful Building Technology

P.O. Box 3866
Missoula, MT 59806
Tel: (406) 549-7678

A guide to inform builders, architects, policy makers, citizens, and homeowners about options presently available in building technology. Updated annually.

Residential Construction Waste Management: A Builder's Field Guide
By Peter Yost & Eric Lund, 1997
NAHB Research Center

Concise source on recycling residential construction wastes.

ReSourceful Specifications: Guideline Specifications for Environmentally Considered Building Materials & Construction Methods
Larry Strain, AIA, Siegel & Strain Architects, 1996.
Siegel & Strain Architects
1295 59th Street
Emeryville, CA 94608
Tel: (510) 547-8092
Fax: (510) 547-2604
E mail: info@siegelstrain.com

Performance specification guidelines on environmental and healthy building materials. It is organized by Construction Specification Institute's (CSI) Divisions 1-16.

The Smart Office: Turning Your Company on Its Head
By A. K. Townsend, 1997
Gila Press
P.O. Box 623
Olney, MD 20830-0478

A guide to making your office healthier and more resource efficient with the goal of increasing profits.

Sustainable Communities: A New Design Synthesis for Cities, Suburbs and Towns
By Sim Van der Ryn & Peter Calthorpe, 1986
Sierra Club
730 Polk Street
San Fransico, CA 94109

A look at sustainable planning that goes beyond mixed-use, high-density, and environmental impact statements and into reverence for nature and a deepening sense of community.

Sustainable Building Technical Manual
Produced by the U.S. Green Building Council, Public Technology Inc. (PTI), and the U.S. Department of Energy, 1996.
U.S Green Building Council
110 Sutter Street, Suite 906
San Francisco, CA 94104

Tel: (415) 445-9500
Fax: (415) 445-9911
E mail: info@usgbc.org
Web site: www.usgbc.org

This practice-oriented manual will provide discussion on green buildings including: significance and environmental impacts of buildings, economics, programming and pre-design, site and building design, construction process, building management, operations & maintenance, and future trends.

WasteSpec: Model Specifications for Construction Waste Reduction, Reuse, and Recycling
by Triangle J Council of Governments
P.O. Box 12276
Research Triangle Park, NC 27709
Tel: (919) 549-0551
Fax: (919) 549-9390
E mail: tjcog@mindspring.com
Web site:
www.tjcog.dst.nc.us/tjcog/

Provides model language to insert in specifications on waste reduction techniques during construction, reuse of construction materials on site, and salvaging and recycling of construction and demolition waste material.

Web Sites

CREST
<www.crest.org>
CREST is a great starting point for any search on energy and sustainability related topics. Among the resources housed are content of the Greening of White House CD-ROM and archives from the green building and straw bale mailing lists.

E-Build.com
Environmental Building News
<www.ebuild.com>
This EBN web site features product reviews, feature articles, and news stories. In addition, the site includes a calendar of events and a bibliography with links for ordering.

Energy Design Resources
<www.energydesignresources.com>
Tools for designers and owners. Comprehensive links site to energy-related organizations.

Greenclips Environmental Journal
<Solstice.crest.org/sustainable/greenclips-info.html>
Editor: Christine Hammer
Biweekly, digital, one-page newsletter
This journal focuses on, sustainable building design, green architecture and related government and buisness issues.

G.E.O Green Building Resource Center
<www.geonetwork.org/gbrc/>
A large collection of sustainability and buildings Internet links, a book list with direct-ordering arrangement through the online bookstore Amazon.com, listings of green designers and other green building professionals, and many other resources.

National Renewable Energy Labs
<www.eren.doe.gov/buildings/tools_directory>
Programs and software tools to help architects, engineers, and code officials evaluate and rank potential energy-efficiency technologies and renewable energy strategies in new or existing buildings.

The U.S. Department of Energy for Sustainability <www.sustainable.doe.gov/> A networking hub for government and private-sector sustainability initiatives. The entire

Sustainable Building Technical Manual is available here as a free download.

What's Working <WhatsWorking.com> Web site for David Johnston, author of this book

Organizations

Council for an Energy Efficient Economy
1001 Connecticut Avenue, N.W., Suite 801
Washington, D.C. 20036
Tel: (202) 429-8873
Web site: aceee.org

Center for Excellence for Sustainable Development
U.S. Department of Energy
1617 Cole Boulevard
Golden, Colorado 80401
Web site:
www.sustainable.doe.gov

Energy Efficient Building Association, Inc. (EEBA)
Northcentral Technical College
1000 Campus
Wausau, WI 544-1
Tel: (715) 675-6331
or
Western Regional Office
6460 N. Mountain View Drive
Parker, CO 80134
Tel: (303) 805-1660

National Association of Home Builders
1201 15th St. NW
Washington, DC 20005
Tel: (800) 368-5242
Fax: (202) 822-0391
Web site: www.nahb.com

National Association of Home Builders Research Center
400 Prince George's Boulevard
Upper Marlboro, MD 20774
Tel: (800) 638-8556
Fax: (301) 249-3265
Web site: www.nahbrc.org

National Fenestration Rating Council
1300 Spring Street, Suite 500
Silver Spring, MD 20910
Tel: (800) WBW-1234
Web site: www.nfrc.org

National Renewable Energy Laboratory (NREL)
1617 Cole Boulevard
Golden, CO 80401
Tel: (303) 275-3000
Web site: www.nrel.gov

Rocky Mountain Institute (RMI)
1739 Snowmass Creek Road
Snowmass, CO 81654
Tel: (970) 927-3420
Web site: www.rmi.org

Sustainable Buildings Industry Council
1331 H St., NW
Suite 1000
Washington, DC 20005-4706
Tel: (202) 628-7400
Web site: www.sbicouncil.org

U.S. Green Buildings Council
1615 L Street NW
Suite 1200
Washington D.C. 20036
Tel: (202) 466-6300
Web site: www.usgbc.org

World Watch Institute
1776 Massachusetts Avenue, NW
Washington, DC 20036
Tel: (202) 452-1999
Fax: (202) 296-7365

Green Builder Programs

Art Castle, Executive Director
HBA of Kitsap County
5251 Auto Center Way
Bremerton, WA 98312-3319
Tel: (360) 479-5778

Program Coordinator
Surburban Maryland BIA
1738 Elton Rd.
Suite 200
Silver Spring, MD 20903
Tel: (301) 445-5400

Kim Calomino, Program Coordinator
HBA of Metropolitan Denver
1400 S. Emerson St.
Denver, CO 80210
Tel: (303) 778-1400
Web site: www.hbadenver.com

Mark Richmond Powers,
Program Coordinator
City of Austin Green Builder Program
206 E. 9th St.
Suite 17102
Austin, TX 78701
Tel: (512) 499-3029
Web site: <www.ci.austin.tx.us/greenbuilder/default.htm>

Karen Snekvik, Executive Director
Clark County HBA
5007 NE St. John's Rd.
Vancouver, WA 98661
Tel: (360) 694-0933

Anna Mayberry, Program Coordinator
HBA of Central New Mexico
5931 Office Blvd. NE
Albequerque, NM 87109
Tel: (505) 344-3294
Web site: www.hbacnm.com

Anthony Floyd, Env. Mgmt. Office
City of Scottsdale
7447 E. Indian School Rd.
Scottsdale, AZ 85251
Tel: (480) 312-4202

Philip Ford
Greater Atlanta HBA
P.O Box 450749
Atlanta, GA 31145-0749
Tel: (720) 938-9900 ext. 20

——— Companies Included in the Book ———

Allen Associates
Dennis Allen, President
1427 Tunnel Road
Santa Barbara, CA 93105
Tel: (805) 682-4305
Fax: (805) 569-6990

Barley & Pfeiffer Architects
Peter Pfeiffer, Principal
1800 W. 6th St.
Austin, TX 78703-4704
Tel: (512) 476-8580
Fax: (512) 476-8667
E mail: greenarchs@aol.com

Bill Eich Construction Co., Inc.
Bill Eich, President
1706 Lincoln Avenue
Spirit lake, IA 51360
Tel: (712) 336-4438
Fax: (712) 336-3962
E mail: billeich@connect.com

ChoicePoint, Inc.
Sue Kertzner, CEO
Ron Kertzner, President
4876 10th St.
Boulder, CO 80304

Dewees Island
John Knott, CEO
46 41st Ave.
Isle of Palms, SC 29451-2662
Tel: (800)-444-7352
Fax: (843) 886-5836
E mail: dewees@mindspring.com
Web site:
www.deweesisland.com

Global Environmental Options
William Reed
4233 Leland
Chevy Chase, MD 20815
Tel: (301) 654-3323

Ideal Homes
Vernon McKown, President
1320 N. Porter
Norman, OK 73071
Tel: (800) 682-2763
Fax: (405) 573-5685

Investec Construction
Jim Van Derhyden, Vice
President
200 E Carillo Ave. # 200
Santa Barbara, CA
Tel: (805) 962-7828
Fax: (805) 962-1918

Kitson Builders
Lee Kitson, President
596 Byrne Ct., NE
Rockford, MI 49431-8400
Tel: (616) 863-9090
Fax: (616) 863-9907

Living Structures, Inc.
Danny Buck, President
1594A San Mateo Ln.
Santa Fe, NM 87505
Tel: (505) 988-2202
Fax: (505) 988-2289
E mail: livingstr@aol.com

McStain Enterprises, Inc.
Tom Hoyt, President
Caroline Hoyt, CEO
Kristen Shewfelt, Market
   Research & Environmental
   Design
75 Manhattan Drive, Suite 1
Boulder, CO 80303-4254
Tel: (303) 494-5900
Fax: (303) 494-9860
E mail: mkr@mcstain.com
Web site: www.mcstain.com

Medallion Homes
John Friesenhann, COO
6929 Camp Bullis Road
San Antonio, TX 78256
Tel: (210) 494-2555
Fax: (210) 494-8109

Sierra Custom Builders
Ronald W. Jones, President
P.O. Box 775
Placitas, NM 87043-0775
Tel: (505) 867-0157
Fax: (505) 344-3103
E mail: ronwjones@juno.com

South Mountain, Co., Inc.
John Abrams, President
P.O. Box 1260
Red Arrow Road
West Tisbury, MA 02575
Tel: (508) 693-4850
Fax: (508) 693-7738

Appendix C
Bibliography

Chapter 1

"Cone/Roper Cause-related Marketing Trends Report 1997."

Edwards, Colleen. *From Good Market Research to Great Marketing: A how-to Guide for Home Builders.* Washington, D.C.: Home Builder Press, 1999.

Gravitz, Alisa. "The Market is Ready for Socially Responsible Business: 44 Million Americans Can't Be Wrong." *Connections* (fall 1997): pp.1-4.

Minton, Ann P. and Randall L. Rose. "The Effects of Environmental Concern on Environmentally Friendly Consumer Behavior: An Exploratory Study." 40 (1997): pp.37-48.

Seiter, Doug. "The Results Are In: Buyers Want Green!" *HomeBuilder.* (September 1999): pp.21-23.

Speer, Tibbett L. "Growing the Green Market." 1997. *American Demographics* (August 1997). 21 July 1999 <http://www.demographics.com/Publications/AD /97ad /9708ad/AD97082.htm>

Chapter 2

Bower, John. *The Healthy Household: A Complete Guide for Creating a Healty Indoor Environment.* Bloomington, IN: The Healthy House Institute, 1995.

Campbell, Colin J. and Jean H. Laherrère. "The End of Cheap Oil." *Scientific American,* March 1998: pp.78-83.

Cunningham, William P. and Barbara Woodworth Saigo. *Environmental Science: A Global Concern.* Dubuque, IA: William C. Brown Publishers, 1997.

Loken, Steve, Rod Minor, and Tracy Mumma. *A Reverence Guide to Resource Efficient Building Elements, 4th ed.* Missoula, MT: Center for Resourceful Building Technology, 1994) p.7.

Marinelli, Janet and Paul Bierman-Lytle. *Your Natural Home: A Complete Source Book and Design Manual for Creating a Healthy, Beautiful, and Environmentally Sensitive House.* New York: Little, Brown and Company, 1995.

National Oceanic and Atmospheric Administration. "Issue of the Global Environmental Change Report." June 14, 1996.

Ott, Wayne, and John Roberts. "Everyday Exposure to Toxic Pollutants," *Scientific American,* February, 1998.

Prowler, Donald. *The Case for the Modest Mansion.* Emmaus PA: Rodale Press, 1986.

Roodman, David Malin and Nicholas Lenssen, "A Building Revolutions: How Ecology and Health concerns are Transforming Construction." Worldwatch Paper 142, March 1995.

Upton, Arthur C. (National Institutes of Health). *Staying Healthy in a Risky Environment.* New York: Simon & Schuster, 1993.

World Resources Institute. "Temperate and Boreal Forests." 21 October 1999 <http://www.wri.org/biodiv/temperat.html>.

Chapter 4

Drucker, Peter F. "Change Leaders." *Inc.* (June 1999): pp.65-72.

Kurtzner, Sue. "The Change Process Model." 1999.

Reed, William G. "The Integrated Design Process." 1999.

Chapter 5

Trellis, Alan. "Managing Your Custom Building Business for Profit." Columbia, MD: Home Builders Network, 1994.